The
Lenten
Pharmacy

The Lenten Pharmacy

Daily
Healing
Therapies

Edward Hays

Forest of Peace Notre Dame, Indiana

© 2006 by Edward M. Hays

Founded in 1865, Ave Maria Press is a ministry of the Indiana Province of Holy Cross.

www.forestofpeace.com

ISBN-10: 0-939516-77-2

ISBN-13: 978-0-939516-77-3

Cover and interior art by Edward M. Hays

Cover and text design by John Carson

Printed and bound in the United States of America.

A Preface
to The Lenten
Pharmacy

Welcome to forty therapeutic days in *The Lenten Pharmacy*. "Therapeutic" may seem an odd adjective for a season that traditionally is observed with fasting, abstinence, and penitential denial. Yet it is appropriate to think of Lent in terms of a pharmacy, which can be either a place or a process of healing, for its origins are from the Greek *pharmakon*, meaning "purification through purging," and *pharmakeia*, meaning "the use of drugs." Indeed, Lent is a healing purge of anything that makes us sick in soul or body. Wholesome healing involves body and soul as a single entity since flesh and spirit are so intimately infused that the affliction of one affects the other.

The word "salvation" originally had secular meanings of freedom and healing, and the same was true of "savior," which comes from the Greek *soter*, meaning "healer." The gospels relate how Jesus as a savior-healer tended sicknesses of body and soul. To say that Jesus is my savior primarily means that he is my healer, physician, and pharmacist. Since disease and sickness have always been with us, pharmaceutical healing arose in the most ancient of societies. The Sumerians, who once lived in present-day Iraq, more than five thousand years ago developed many of our still-existing medical treatments, including inhalations, pills, enemas, infusions, lotions, ointments, and even the equivalent of our modern aspirin, in the form of natural willow bark.

The symbols used for pharmacy include a large letter R, with its right leg crossed by a slanted bar. ℞ The most frequent explanation for this symbol is that it is an abbreviation of the Latin *recipere* or "recipe," meaning "take thou." In former times the Latin *fiat mistura*, meaning "let a mixture be made," followed this. The grinding of herbs and drugs required the skill of a pharmacist, whose mixing bowl and pestle have become symbols of this profession. As late as 1920, druggists ground and mixed 80 percent of the prescriptions they filled, but by 1971 that number had decreased to 1 percent or less. Not until the 1800s was a medical distinction made between an apothecary and pharmacist, who mixes medicines, and a physician or doctor, who treats a patient with medicine.

The Lenten Pharmacy is a manual of medicinal reflections on Jesus, the Galilean Healer's prescriptions for alleviating the various crippling afflictions of body and soul. These daily reflections include Jesus' instructions for how to live a healthy and holy life. Some of these prescriptions will seem difficult or unpalatable, like bitter medicine. But all will lead to real and abundant life. May the following ancient and new prescriptions aid the healing of your body and spirit as you visit daily your lenten pharmacy.

℞ PREFACE TO THE LENTEN PHARMACY

ASH WEDNESDAY

Today your lenten pharmacy offers the remedial application of inert gray ashes. Not normally used as a medicine, the seemingly useless residue of a fire warrants a closer look as a possible pharmaceutical treatment.

For the ancients, ashes vividly symbolized what results when the life-fire has departed from a body. This stark image of death was reflected in the ritual words used upon administering blessed ashes in ages past: *Pulvis es, in pulverem reverteris*—"Dust thou art, and to dust thou shall return." Lent itself was originally a penitential season of reconciliation with the church—ashes and sackcloth being the visible signs of repentant sinners who were seeking public reunion with the church. Along with fasting, ashes were a sign of mourning and grief at times of death. In times of disaster, they served as physical offerings of supplication to God. Christian ascetics used to sprinkle ashes on their food to indicate their total disdain for the pleasures of the body. The ancient Mayans of Central America used ashes as an inoculation against disease, much like a flu shot. When planting corn, they mixed in ashes to protect their seeds from blight and rotting.

Now, you are not a sinner seeking public reconciliation and quite likely you are not planting corn or mourning the death of a loved one, so how can today's ashes be good medicine for you? You can start by letting today's ashes vaccinate your seeds of reform against maggot "tomorrowitis," that procrastination fungus that postpones a reform of life until next year's Lent or even until your deathbed. The pharmacist-healer Jesus says to all those suffering from lethargic encephalitis, the deadening inflammation of the brain that is so common in our culture: "Stay awake. Seek healing this very day, for you do not know if you will be alive tomorrow. Now is the hour to awaken."

Ashes are also an ageless remedy for sickly prayer. Abraham of old practiced this prayer remedy when he said, "Let me take it upon myself to speak to my Lord, I who am but dust and ashes" (Gn 18:27). When daring to beg favors from the Undying Font of Mercy, Abraham laced his humble prayer with the ashes of his own grave. Lying in the dust of one's death-rest is an antidote to the hubris and hyperactivity that mark our contemporary way of life. Praying from such a position of humility heals the soul with true justification—just as it did for the tax collector praised by Jesus in the parable of the Pharisee and the tax collector:

> The tax collector, standing far off, would not even look up to heaven, but was beating his breast and saying, "God, be merciful to me, a sinner!"   —Lk 18:13

Here is a good Ash Wednesday prescription: Slowly read aloud this parable of Jesus found in Luke 18:9–14.

℞ ASH WEDNESDAY

Because of infirmity, family obligations, or work-related responsibilities, you may not be able to go to church today and be marked with ashes. But do not let that prevent you from being touched by this powerful ancient medicine. All the earth is holy land and its soil is blessed. So, place a small pinch of dust or dirt in the palm of your hand and use it to trace upon yourself the sign of the cross, a sign of death that leads to new life, as you prayerfully ask God to heal you.

ASH WEDNESDAY

ASH THURSDAY

The real sign of Lent is not ashes but the cross. Every cross echoes Jesus' challenge: "If any want to become my followers, let them deny themselves and take up their cross and follow me" (Mk 8:34). The Romans reserved the wooden cross, an instrument of excruciating pain and shame, as capital punishment for the lowest of criminals, revolutionaries, and terrorists. Yet, at five different times, Jesus tells his followers to take up their crosses. It's hard to imagine that he would have had more than a mere handful of followers if his listeners thought that he was referring to the hideously painful Roman cross.

Some scripture scholars believe that Jesus was speaking of a cross other than the Roman cross. In *Treasures Old and New*, Gail Ramshaw writes of the curative properties of the last letter in the Hebrew alphabet, *Tau*, a letter shaped like our English *T*. Jewish tradition holds that at the Exodus, the Israelites traced the sign of the *Tau* in lamb's blood on their door posts as a symbol of God's protection and life. The prophet Ezekiel said that those whose foreheads were marked with the *Tau* would be strengthened to remain faithful through the harsh difficulties of the End Times (Ez 9:4). Those protectively signed with the *Tau* cross were already prophetically living in the New Reign of God. Indeed, Jesus transformed the Roman cross, the wooden cross he carried and upon which he died, into a *Tau* cross, a cross of blessing, healing, and protection. Today, when Jesus invites us to take up our crosses and follow him, when we are asked to embrace some painful, personal difficulty in our lives, we can do so in a radically new and pharmaceutical way.

The *Tau* cross was a powerful healing sign of God's liberating us from bondage, of the grace of endurance in difficult times, and of the glorious freedom of those already living in the reign of God. Consider tracing the *Tau* cross on your forehead when you begin praying or in a difficult situation when you feel like throwing in the towel. Use this potent sign of the cross whenever you are tempted to abandon your lenten resolutions because they seem too difficult. Creatively alternate the traditional sign of the cross with making the *Tau* cross. As a full body ritual, begin the *Tau* cross not on your forehead, but at the top of your chest near your heart, then move down to your waist, then from shoulder to shoulder. To remind yourself of all the associations of the *Tau* cross, you could substitute for the names of the Trinity, "God's Freedom, Fidelity, Love, and Peace."

This Lent consider making a simple *Tau* cross for your home or prayer place; it might be made of cardboard or constructed from two pieces of wood. Let your *Tau* cross remind you daily of Ezekiel's prophecy that those who bore this sign were living ahead of their time. Let your *Tau* cross challenge you to live fearlessly, with the uncommon and blessed awareness of one for whom the radical New Age, the Kingdom of God, has already arrived.

Ash Thursday

ASH
FRIDAY

"**K**now your pet faults" is among the many practical pieces of advice contained in a small gift booklet for graduating college seniors who are about to begin a new stage in life. "Pet" is an unusual, even shocking, adjective for personal failings, as it is a term usually reserved for tame animals treated with affection. Pet is also slang for someone's favorite person or a pampered love. So, know your pampered faults!

Lent sneaks up on us as our lives are crowded with work and social activities and cluttered with commitments. As a result, we're usually unprepared for the soul work of these forty days. So, on this first lenten Friday take paper and pen and make a list of your pet faults or vices. It can be a spiritual health self-examination to list those domesticated personal faults you treat with affection instead of chastisement.

Jesus said, "Those who are well have no need of a physician, but those who are sick do" (Mk 2:17). If you're not sick, you don't need the Healer and you don't need Lent! This year, instead of simply falling back on the usual lenten acts of fasting or attending devotions, decide to treat with healing discipline your pampered faults. Turn every pet vice

ASH FRIDAY

inside out or upside down; treat your illness by doing the opposite. If you are so cautious with your money as to be stingy (and proud of your prudence), then your healing prescription is to exercise large doses of generosity as a lenten work. If you pamper yourself and protect yourself from the outcast, the hungry, and the homeless, you might volunteer to serve a meal at a soup kitchen.

Lent is only for the sick! So, if you find that the page of paper on which you listed your pet faults is empty, ask someone with whom you live or work to name your pet faults, since their eyesight is better than yours is! As you examine your faults and reflect on possible prescriptions, include the five famous ideal works on God's list found in today's reading from Isaiah 58:6–87:

> Is not this the fast that I choose: to loose the
> bonds of injustice, to undo the thongs of the
> yoke, to let the oppressed go free, and to break
> every yoke? Is it not to share your bread with
> the hungry, and bring the homeless poor into
> your house . . . ?

Isaiah ends this list of what constitutes the kind of fasting God truly desires by speaking like a physician. He says that when you care for the poor, hungry, and needy your light will break forth like the dawn, and your wound will quickly be healed! That mysterious "wound" of which Isaiah speaks is that which most cries out to be healed in each of us. Time-release medicines are often prescribed today. It may be that Jesus, the Mystic Physician, performs a time-release healing of our mysterious wound, a cure that we only become aware of after we die. But even if we are not fully aware of our healing until heaven, let us practice faithfully our lenten prescriptions so that the hidden light breaking forth within us will heal our wounds.

ASH FRIDAY

ASH
SATURDAY

"**T**ake this medicine on Sunday" is the message printed on the prescription label of today's bitter lenten medicine. Saturday, the original Sabbath—the day of relaxation and leisure—ranks as one of the superior medicines of the ancient world. But an entire day of rest and leisure in our restless, compulsively active world might be for some of us as excruciatingly painful as stomach surgery without any anesthesia! Hectic work schedules, social obligations, various church activities, and endless athletic events create unfinished household tasks that often twist Sundays into workdays so that we can try to accomplish all that we think is necessary. Recent research shows that the average American works at least 350 hours more per year than does the average European. Americans also suffer significantly more from cardiac arrest, cancer, and stress-related illnesses than do Europeans.

Originally, the Sabbath rest was a weekly Fourth of July holiday to remind the Israelites that before their exodus they had been Egyptian slaves, forced to labor endlessly, seven days a week. If you are searching for a good lenten resolution,

ASH SATURDAY

consider making tomorrow and every lenten Sunday a real Sabbath by doing nothing practical. The unrelenting stress and tension that causes many of our psychological and physical sicknesses could find a cure in a weekly holiday—free from work, a true Sabbath day of rest. In today's reading Isaiah quotes God:

> If you refrain from trampling the Sabbath, from pursuing your own interests on my holy day; if you call the Sabbath a delight . . . then you shall take delight in the Lord.
> —Isaiah 58:13–14

And those who delight God by sharing bread with the hungry and observing the Sabbath are promised the following medicinal cures:

> The Lord will guide you continually, and satisfy your needs in parched places, and make your bones strong; and you shall be like a watered garden, like a spring of water, whose waters never fail.
> —Isaiah 58:11

While the FDA might question such lavish health claims, know that this prescription bears the gold seal of a divine guarantee.

A symptom of Sabbath dis-ease, that restlessness of always having to be productive or busy, is finding your wellsprings bone dry! The draining, relentless pressure of constantly working, whether at your job or at home, siphons away life-

ASH SATURDAY

giving resilience and creates a joyless desert in life and in lovemaking. Healing is found in a weekly vacation day of leisure. Still, while clearly medicinal, many would find a weekly day of leisure to be more of a curse than a blessing and the majority would say that it is, quite frankly, impossible! Yet some healing is better than no healing, so seriously consider taking this lenten prescription: "Take at least a half a dose of Sabbath once a week—and begin this healing medicine tomorrow!"

ASH SATURDAY

THE FIRST
WEEK
OF LENT

FIRST SUNDAY
IN LENT

In today's gospel reading, Jesus, led by the Spirit of God, walks away from his work and responsibilities to take the desert cure (see Mk 1:12–15). A Palestinian proverb in his day was "Physician, heal thyself," and by this withdrawal into the wilderness we might wonder if Jesus is seeking the healing of desert medicine. Alone in the desolate wilderness inhabited by evil spirits and wild beasts, without food or water, and stripped of the security of his fellow villagers and companions, God alone becomes his sustenance! It appears that the desert purges Jesus of the infection of self-sufficiency; indeed, from that time onward God is the sole source of his strength. For Jesus, desert isolation is a *pharmakon*, as it forces him to confront his utter dependency on God. Independence comes only with adulthood and is a goal we work hard to reach. Yet independence can be like an eye infection, blinding us to the reality that even our every breath is dependent upon God, the source of all life.

Jesus began his teaching by saying, "The time is fulfilled, and the kingdom of God has come near; repent, and believe in the good news"(Mk 1:15). Good doctors take their own medicine. By going into the wilderness and purging himself of his family and village support system, Jesus learned to trust in

God as a continuously caring, protecting, and loving parent. We proudly independent Americans find purging ourselves of independence painfully difficult and logically ask, "Isn't there an easier way?" The answer comes in the words of the former British prime minister, Margaret Thatcher, whose favorite response to her objectors was: "TINA," There Is No Alternative.

Lent is TINA time. There is no alternative to Jesus' requirements to repent—to turn around—and believe in the good news; that is, if you wish to be his disciple. Conversion is no brief forty-day exercise; it is a lifetime practice of returning/repenting that requires an ongoing bit-by-bit purging of anything in us that isn't godly. On Ash Friday, you were invited to make a list of your pet faults. Now, on this first Sunday of Lent, make a list of three pet self-set limitations. These growth boundaries mark how you've embraced or settled for who you are instead of seeking who you can become.

Lent is the season of becoming and of removing the restrictive boundaries that seriously limit our growth, the fullness of life, and the depths of our souls. On this desert Sunday, begin purging your pet limitations as well as those self-established boundaries you have placed on your prayer, patience, forgiveness, generosity, and care of the poor.

THE FIRST WEEK OF LENT

Monday of the First Week in Lent

The desert cure that the Lenten Pharmacist proposes today is an over-the-counter drug, castor oil. Purging involves ridding the body of toxic elements; it's a process that is essential for maintaining health. As a drug, castor oil is bitter tasting, and Egyptian physicians mixed honey with it to make it more palatable. The taste problem was creatively resolved in 1905 by a Hungarian immigrant druggist named Max Kiss, who created the chocolate flavored medicine Ex-Lax.

Because an authentic lenten purging of negative habits and addictive behavior is so distasteful, we often seek easy Ex-Lax solutions, such as abstaining from meat on Fridays, fasting from sweets, or some other pious practice. Pharmacist Jesus, however, after emerging from his desert Lent, was well aware that there's no easy-to-swallow chocolate-covered conversion and so prescribed the bitter medicine of "Reform your lives!" He could have added, "just as I have reformed (radically altered) my life." Returning to Nazareth after his baptism and desert retreat, Jesus was a changed man. No longer the quiet village carpenter, he became a prophet, powerful in word and deed.

Good physicians take their own medicine. So what was it that Jesus administered to himself that so radically altered his life? The scriptures are silent. Yet the wilderness may hold the answer to this mystery, for Mark tells us that in the desert Jesus was with wild beasts. His was no directed retreat; he read no scriptures or spiritual books, nor did he listen to taped sermons of holy rabbis—it was just solitude and wild beasts.

Did the silence of solitude purge him of the continuous racket and idle babbling of his village life? Isn't that what made it possible for him to hear the tiny, quiet voice of God speaking within him? And did the vacuum of solitude open his eyes to the presence of the inner wild beasts that he was forced to confront? Being fully human, Jesus had to wrestle with human impatience, anger, pride, and the hunger for fame or power. Yet wild beasts can be tamed—with patience and love—and, once tamed, they can become our powerful allies.

We avoid the distasteful lenten laxative of solitude because of what questions—and wild beasts—we, like Jesus, may have to confront. As we seek an easy Ex-Lax Lent, Jesus the Galilean Pharmacist says, "Do not be afraid to take this powerful and ancient medicine. I assure you from personal experience that it is truly an excellent cure."

THE FIRST WEEK OF LENT

TUESDAY OF THE FIRST WEEK IN LENT

By the fourth century, the once dynamic body of Christianity was diagnosed to be anemic, after having diluted itself as the official religion of the Roman Empire. Wishing to heal themselves of this lukewarm virus, a few reformers took the desert cure by retreating to the sandy wilderness of Egypt and Palestine to find what Jesus found in his wilderness times. Heroic men and women fled the cities for the desert, seeking to enkindle that former zeal for gospel holiness. The wilderness medicine worked. Living as hermits, these desert fathers and mothers purged themselves of the luxuries and comforts of city life and found God in their solitude and prayer. Their insightful writings became the first spiritual guides for a long contemplative tradition in Christianity. Yet, as with all zealous movements, there were extremists among them who, living alone without fraternal correction, engaged in often bizarre and even harmful penances.

A hundred years or so later, St. Benedict of Nursia, seeking this desert holiness without having to go to the wilderness of Egypt, began the movement of western monasticism. The benefits of the desert could now be experienced inside the walls of monasteries in the mountains of Italy. These monastic walled-in deserts provided a sanctuary from the pleasures of the city and the self-limiting conflicts and structures of the world and family life. Monasticism provided a rule of life for those seeking holiness, with set times of communal prayer and work, and with fasting, celibacy, and bodily penances in moderation. To this day, monasticism remains the classical model of prayer and holiness for religious men and women, for the secular clergy, and for many lay people.

The most frequently proposed religious practices during Lent often seem designed more for a monastery than for the marketplace. Monastic spirituality is a rich and valuable way of holiness, but it is not a practical path for typical twenty-first-century city dwellers. Daily obligations around work and family do not allow the luxury of retreating from urban clamor to find God in the solitude and meditation that are provided in cloistered seclusion. Some seventeen centuries after the desert mothers and fathers, we have yet to recognize as authentic an urbanized or suburbanized lay spirituality.

Since our Jewish ancestors were wandering desert nomads, biblical texts abound with references to the desert as God's dwelling place. Our task, then, is to discover God's abiding presence everywhere in the world. God's presence permeates a noisy, bustling marketplace or a raucous home filled with small children just as much as it does an isolated wilderness or a medieval monastery. Jesus affirmed that sacred reality. He never calls us to retreat from the marketplace or the world but medicinally invites us to discover within it the abiding divine presence. Make your lenten work of this day an exploration of, and a dwelling in, the mystical reign of God that Jesus said was among us here and now.

THE FIRST WEEK OF LENT

Wednesday of the First Week in Lent

Baptism gave birth to the first Lent. After his life-altering baptism by John, the Spirit of God escorted Jesus into the desert to spend a prolonged period reflecting on what had happened to him. That same Holy Spirit is eager to lead you into the desert of this lenten season, where you can pharmaceutically reflect upon your awesome baptism, whether you were baptized as an infant or an adult. The renowned scripture scholar Raymond Brown reminds us that the day of our baptism is more significant than the day of a wedding or ordination to the priesthood or the episcopacy! Lent should awaken us to our rarely exercised, or even perceived, priestly and prophetic anointing as baptized disciples of the risen Christ. We glory in the awesome dignity of baptism.

Every baptized priestly woman and man should be a person of prayer. Urban-dwelling disciples today are challenged to create a lifestyle of municipal meditation. The silence of a monastic cloister or a Zen temple is conducive to meditative prayer. On the other hand, a noisy, horn-honking traffic jam or a rattling, crowded subway is more conducive to municipal centrifugal prayer. Unlike centering prayer, where the movement is centripetal—inward to encounter the mystery of God—centrifugal prayer spins outward from the center of the self, whirling out into the world like the spiraling arms of a galaxy.

Centering prayer flows out of the monastic tradition and is based on the indwelling of the Divine. With eyes closed and silently repeating a mantra or focusing word, one strives to empty the mind of all thoughts so as to experience God in the stillness of the present moment. Centrifugal prayer, on the other hand, is based on an equally true reality—the ever-present dwelling of the Divine Mystery in all places. In this meditation, we keep our eyes open in order to fill our heart, mind, and soul with the invisible Divine Presence in which we are being engulfed. In an act of faith-filled adoration, we can acknowledge this presence of God with a slight nod or bow of reverence made to the flat tire, or to the jammed traffic beginning to move once again, or to the gift of an empty parking space.

Rich and healthy is the person who is able to pray both centering and centrifugal prayer since they perfectly complement one another. In many ways, centering prayer is easier, as the distracting exterior world has been shut out and the voice of God can be heard more clearly. For most of us, municipal meditation or centrifugal prayer is more difficult, demanding more faith because the congestion, pandemonium, and bedlam of city and suburban life easily eclipse the presence of God. Yet, both the busy urbanite and the cloistered monk or nun are called to holiness by union with God in the midst of daily life. The good news of the gospel is that it is just as valid to be a municipal saint as it is to be a monastic one.

THE FIRST WEEK OF LENT

THURSDAY OF THE FIRST WEEK IN LENT

Mother Teresa, renowned for her tender care of India's sick and dying, once said, "The biggest disease today is not leprosy or tuberculosis, but rather the disease of being unwanted!" Her diagnosis of the world's greatest plague calls us to be doctors without borders, healers of a global sickness.

In today's gospel (Mt 7:7–12), Matthew quotes Jesus saying that all the commandments can be summarized in this: "Do unto others as you would have them do to you" (Mt 7:13). For municipal disciples of the Healer-Savior, the term "treating others" holds a playful, but powerful, double meaning. The first meaning is to show others the same behavior as we would want shown to us. A physician's use of the term "treat" adds the sense that we are to attend to others' wounds, as we would wish to be cared for if we were sick. Let your lenten reflection today be to ponder your personal response to Mother Teresa's diagnosis of the world's greatest epidemic, whose walking-afflicted you encounter daily. Baptism has made healers of us all.

Doctor Jesus used the ancient medicine of love and respect to treat the undesirables who were exiled to the far edges of his society—sinners, prostitutes, tax collectors, and the religious lepers snubbed by the righteous for their failure to observe every minute religious law. Sick people are contagious, so the seemingly prudent keep a proper distance from them lest they become polluted with the same disease. Jesus didn't keep such a prophylactic distance from the sickly unwanted ones, nor did he wear plastic gloves while eating with prostitutes to protect his reputation as a holy man. Being a wise physician of the spirit, he knew the cure worked only by direct, physical, and loving contact.

In baptism, through our unity with Christ the Savior, we were anointed as priests and prophets and also as healers. Unlike Jesus, as you make your daily rounds you will probably not encounter social-religious castoffs, prostitutes, or corrupt tax collectors. You will, however, come into direct contact with those who feel insignificant, unwanted, or of little value. These are the invisible people; they may be sackers at the grocery store, garbage collectors, the homeless, or those on welfare. This sickness of unimportance especially infects teenagers who lack the gifts of athletic ability, a high IQ, or good looks. The disease of being unwanted afflicts the elderly in nursing homes and the aged living alone in their homes. On this day and in the coming days of Lent, make it your practice to practice the healing medicine of Jesus and Mother Teresa.

THE FIRST WEEK OF LENT

Friday of the First Week in Lent

Jesus went off into the wilderness, a word that comes from the Old English *wilddeor*, meaning "wild animals." Mark wisely told us that Jesus "was among wild beasts" and Matthew adds that in this wilderness he also encountered the devil, the personification of evil. So, be prepared in these days of your lenten retreat for such encounters with the untamed beasts and the evil that dwell in you and around you.

The perpetual presence of evil in the world is an undeniable reality that reveals its dark self in our personal sins and in what Peter Gomes calls "the sins of the system." These communal or cultural sins of a society or nation include war, slavery, legalized racial and sexual discrimination, and the ruthless profit-driven exploitation of the poor, migrants, and the uneducated.

The concept of corporate sin is both ancient and new. Most examinations of conscience dwell only on personal sins and faults, yet we are also accountable for those actions done in our name as a nation. Vocally denouncing and objecting to immoral national acts and policies certainly reduces our personal moral liability, but to what degree such moral protest absolves us is something only God can judge. Each citizen of a nation harvests the good or evil seeds that the country sows.

Sin is sickness, a pestilence that infects both the individual and the social system. While our American society may seem like a faceless entity, it is composed of individuals with real faces—and souls. Just as we are personally responsible for our sins, so we are communally accountable for the sins of our nation, especially if we support those sins and the leaders who enact them.

Last Friday we were encouraged to make a list of our pet faults. Today, make a short list of your pet virtues. The medicinal reason for compiling this brief index of your best qualities is critical since your virtue is the weakest part of your soul's immune system. Being diabolically clever, evil cunningly attacks where you are the weakest, which is paradoxically where you feel the strongest and most virtuous. For example, virtuous weekly church attendance can reassure us that we are fulfilling our religious duties and so can camouflage our failures in generously caring for the poor and oppressed. Likewise, the virtue of patriotism, while praiseworthy as a love of our native country, can easily blind us to the immoral sins of our country, such as war and the ruthless pursuit of financial gain. Similarly, the praiseworthy virtue of promptness is fertile soil for sins of impatience, anger, and resentment.

Today, make a short list of your pet virtues, those qualities for which you will be praised at your funeral. Then post an alert lenten guard at those unprotected strongholds to guard against sneak assaults by the Evil One.

THE FIRST WEEK OF LENT

SATURDAY OF THE FIRST WEEK IN LENT

Tomorrow is Ketchup Sunday! For overworked, busy 24/7 Americans, Sunday is a second Saturday—a catch-up day—required for mowing the lawn, shopping, cleaning, and doing the laundry. Regardless of the constitutional separation of church and state, many Americans proudly proclaim that "America is a Christian nation." This religious myth is used to defend erecting monuments of the Ten Commandments in public places. Yet what best defines America as a Christian nation? Is it having the Ten Commandments in our public institutions or having the majority of our citizens faithfully adhere to them, including the third commandment, "Thou shalt keep holy the Lord's Day"?

Today continues last Saturday's reflection on Lent as a time for a healing rejuvenation of Sunday as a day of leisure and rest. To attend worship for an hour on the first day of the week isn't enough; lenten resolutions should heal our wounds and not just superficially salve them. Scripture scholars say that worship attendance at the synagogue during the time of Jesus was not a requirement for the Sabbath, but rest from work was. The Mosaic Law defined that the way to keep the Sabbath holy was by abstaining from labor. Attendance at weekly worship can help us enter into Sabbath rest but by itself doesn't allow the Sabbath's curative benefits to take hold.

Our Sundays need to be designed as a lively tonic to restore the tired and weary. Pharmacies in the ancient world offered various salves and ointments for such rejuvenation. A good prescription for sick Sundays is scribbling on your calendar after each Sunday the word "*Sabbat*," making it the hybrid "Sunday-*Sabbat*!" In Hebrew, *Sabbat* means "to rest," and so the first day of the week would become "Sunday-to Rest." After a long week of work, following this simple scribbled prescription can work healing miracles, by rejuvenating you personally as well as revitalizing your marriage and family. Rest has medicinal power, and rest at home can heal you with the aids of relaxation, reading, enjoying a hobby, or reconnecting with nature. Today's dire poverty of leisure is injurious to the love relationships of friends, spouses, parents, and children, causing each of us to be locked inside our own whirling hamster cages, endlessly running from one thing to another.

Yet for all its benefits, abstaining from labor on your Sunday-Sabbath may be as difficult as it is for alcoholics to give up liquor. To help you break your addiction to work, you might begin to think of the Sunday-Sabbath as a weekly mini-vacation. When you're sick and tired of the old, endless grind with no light at the end of the tunnel, rejoice that God wants to give you fifty-two weekly free days a year—on top of your annual vacation!

THE FIRST WEEK OF LENT

THE SECOND
WEEK
OF LENT

SECOND SUNDAY IN LENT

Pharmacies or drug stores have entire departments devoted exclusively to one of the oldest of all healing medicines—cosmetics! In Egypt over 8,000 years ago, these cures included a variety of skin creams and oils, rouges for cheeks, and coloring tints for skin, lips, and hair—for use by the living and for the dead. "Cosmetics," which comes from the Greek word for "skilled in decorating," are medicines designed to treat the disease of aging and that equally ancient affliction of not being beautiful enough. These disguising ointments attempt to restore what time has stolen: youthfulness, sexual vigor, flesh tone, and hair.

In ancient times, men used cosmetic cures for hair more than women did. One prescription for male baldness was a paste of crushed myrtle berries and bear grease. Graying hair was treated by wearing a paste of herbs and earthworms overnight! While dark or black hair was common in Mediterranean societies, blond hair was considered more beautiful because it was associated with Greek heroes like Achilles. The prescription for golden blond hair was to use yellow flower pollen, yellow flour, and even fine gold dust or bleaches from Phoenicia.

THE SECOND WEEK OF LENT

To our knowledge, Jesus of Nazareth didn't use cosmetics, yet he could have since he was relatively old when he began his public ministry at about the age of thirty. Jesus was likely older than his disciples and the majority of those who encountered him because in Palestine at that time 75 percent of the population died by their mid-twenties. Those who lived beyond that age commonly suffered from tooth loss and a variety of diseases. By the age of forty, 90 percent were dead. So the Jesus who climbed that high mountain could well have been an aged, wrinkled, graying man, yet he was transfigured more gloriously than a youthful, golden-haired Greek god-hero. Is the transfiguration that we hear about in today's gospel (Mk 9:2–10) just a preview of the heavenly glory we shall share with the Risen Christ, or does it have some personal meaning for this life?

Everyone suffers from the effects of aging, and while cosmetics can hide and reduce these effects, is there another art or "skill in decorating"? Lent is a cosmetic season to beautify not only the outside but also the inside. Our lenten practices are intended to allow what is inside to radiate outward, as Jesus did when he became the transparent, see-through Christ. But, you object, he was the Son of God! True, but does not the glorious image of God also reside in you? Perhaps like dull, old silver, the image has lost its luster— tarnished by neglect, sins, and human frailties. Prayer polishes the soul and a habitual desire for inner beauty causes your soul to surface splendidly on your face in a radiant smile. Your transfiguration into the glorious Christ need not be delayed until death. Simply begin today to think, to speak, and to act as he did.

THE SECOND WEEK OF LENT

MONDAY OF THE SECOND WEEK IN LENT

If we could have shared with those three disciples the mystical experience of the transfiguration of Jesus, how different would our Lent and our lives be! The Islamic spiritual teacher Ibn Al-Arabi taught that spiritual seekers have a religious duty to create imaginative theophanies—appearances of God—for themselves. I believe he uses the strong expression "religious duty" because second- or third-hand religious experiences simply don't transform or inspire. If, indeed, it is your religious duty, then consider making one of your lenten activities the creation of your own mystical visions. This isn't pretending or a make-believe mysticism of seeing what isn't there. Rather, it is using our God-given imagination to make present the sacred unseen. That awesome divine mystery is present everywhere in creation but is too dangerous to be seen with our normal vision. Yet, it can be safely imagined by our mind's eye.

The theophany of the burning bush, out of which Moses heard God speaking to him, is a good model for us. Choose any common bush or tree and set it aflame with your imagination; then, listen for what you might hear. You don't need a mountaintop to have a mystical experience; your laundry room will do just fine. As you remove freshly cleaned clothing from the dryer, see it as dazzlingly white as Jesus' clothes at the Transfiguration. Albert Einstein said, "The most beautiful and most profound emotion we can experience is the sensation of the mystical . . . he (she) who can no longer wonder and stand rapt in awe, is as good as dead." Mystical experiences, then, are not superfluous to life but are essential to living it fully.

There's an old saying: "What do you do after a mystical experience? You do the laundry!" To this I would add, "but you do it differently!" With your imagination, the finger of God's spirit, you can creatively illustrate images of yourself as a kinder, friendlier, more prayerful, compassionate, and patient person. Dwell upon these images of yourself with a zealous desire that they be realized. Then, let that holy finger of God's spirit prod you forward into actualizing those mental pictures in your daily life.

As we create our mental blueprints for personal reform—for becoming better and more lovable people—it is crucial to remember that it isn't necessary to make ourselves more lovable in order to be acceptable to God. To be lovingly accepted by God doesn't require removing a single fault, yet God's love for us urges and enables their removal. Jesus' invitation to discipleship did not require that those who wanted to follow him be sinless, pure, or perfect. He simply said, "Come, follow me," knowing that in so doing they would be transfigured into beautiful, living images of the All Beautiful One. In other words, freedom from sin is a fruit of faithful Christian discipleship, not its prerequisite.

THE SECOND WEEK OF LENT

TUESDAY OF THE SECOND WEEK IN LENT

Pharmacies do not sell placebos, but perhaps they should. Those sugar pills, lacking any medicinal substances, sometimes produce surprisingly healing effects. European physicians and neurologists in the late nineteenth century began prescribing these imaginary medicines to treat imaginary illnesses. In their medical practices, they encountered patients suffering from a variety of painful symptoms, yet clinical tests revealed no verifiable physical causes of the symptoms. The physicians concluded that their patients' afflictions were the result of hysteria created by repressed anxieties and suppressed feelings. When they prescribed placebos, telling patients that they were taking a new, powerful medicine, astounding recoveries often occurred.

The healing achieved by this imaginative medicine demonstrates the ability of the mind to create both illness and healing. The power of belief to produce physical changes was clearly and humorously shown in experiments where people acted drunk after taking what they believed was strong liquor but in reality was only placebo alcohol. After Jesus had cured someone, he frequently said, "Your faith has healed you" (Mk 10:52) Interestingly, some translations use "saved" instead of "healed," as both are implied in the root word. All this suggests the profound importance of faith in your personal healing and in your lenten practices. If you take some daily medication, think about the healthy practice of the Hopi Indians of the Southwest, who say that all medicine should be taken with a prayer. Be your own pharmacist, lovingly mixing together your medicines with trust-filled prayer, and you will find the effectiveness of your medicine to be greatly enhanced.

The best prescriptions for ensuring good physical health always include a proper diet and regular exercise. Because what we think impacts our well-being in both body and soul, it is also essential to maintain a proper diet of wholesome thoughts. Such a diet should include blessings and good wishes for all people and thoughts of gratitude for the gifts of life and the beauties of creation. A healthy diet also abstains from sickening thoughts of anger, revenge, hatred, and violence. A mental diet devoid of such thoughts is especially difficult in our culture, because we Americans seem addicted to violence in our sports, our entertainment, and even in the way we resolve our international conflicts. With our thoughts we make our world. One has to wonder if we are creating this cultural creed:

> We believe violent words or deeds are the best way to resolve interpersonal and domestic conflicts.
> We believe violent behavior on the sports field or in the movies is fun and good entertainment.

THE SECOND WEEK OF LENT

> We believe armed intervention in global
>> conflicts is more noble than patient
>> diplomacy and, therefore, the best course
>> of action.

This second Tuesday of Lent is a good day to begin to reshape our cultural creed so that it more closely reflects the Apostles' Creed. If we follow today's prescription of imagining ourselves into better spiritual health, then perhaps at the end of Lent Jesus will say to us, "Your faith has healed you."

THE SECOND WEEK OF LENT

WEDNESDAY OF THE SECOND WEEK IN LENT

Was Jesus a quack doctor since he never attended medical school? Self-promoting charlatans eagerly peddling cure-all medicines are called quacks, which is an abbreviation of quacksalver. "Quack," of course, is the sound a duck makes, and "salve" refers to medicine. Fake healers were also known as "medicine men" in the mid-1800s when they sold patent medicines in sideshows. But Jesus isn't a quacksalver or a quacksavior! In Mark's gospel, not only does Jesus make no wild claims, but he is reluctant even to heal, and those whom he did heal were told not to tell anyone about it.

Interestingly, Jesus never said, "I healed you," but rather told people, "Your faith has healed you." He intimately involved the sick in their recovery by drawing out their belief that they could be healed. Congregational pastor Donna Schaper says that these words of Jesus suggest that wellness actually may be the capacity to trust. Such wellness requires a mature faith, not in miracles but in the living marvel of the body's divinely embedded health. Human wellness may be facilitated by prescribed medicines, but it remains both a physical and a spiritual issue. Jesus, as a good healer, treated body and soul as one. He healed people rather than curing them—and there is a big difference!

Many years ago, I saw a motion picture about Jesus of Nazareth. In the movie, a Roman man goes to a small Palestinian village to find a paralyzed woman who is reported to have been cured by Jesus. He finds a joyful and beautiful young woman, who, to his dismay, is still paralyzed and unable to walk. When he asks her if she is indeed the one whom Jesus cured, she replies, "Yes, I am the one the Master healed. I am no longer paralyzed, as I once was, with angry resentment at being a cripple." The crippled woman had been healed spiritually, the more profound of her maladies.

Today's assignment is to give yourself a physical-spiritual exam to see if while being physically healthy, you are somehow spiritually sick or paralyzed—unable to be free. Yesterday's reflection on the power of our beliefs and thoughts can be helpful in detecting thoughts that may be paralyzing you, even if you appear to be in good health. Once you have diagnosed the source of your problem, prescribe your own remedial medicine to remove what causes your poor spiritual health.

If your examination shows that you enjoy true wellness— even if you suffer from arthritis, heart problems, or another illness—follow the example of the healed Samaritan leper and give lavish thanks to God for healing you. Those who truly enjoy wellness while being sick are easily recognized: They are pleasant, happy, and free of complaints. They focus not on their own needs but on the needs of others, and they passionately resist canonizing themselves as living martyrs of the cross.

THE SECOND WEEK OF LENT

THURSDAY OF THE SECOND WEEK IN LENT

Some of us find physical exercise as distasteful as bitter medicine. A recent survey revealed that over 60 percent of Americans do not exercise. While medical results have proven that exercise improves one's immune system, controls weight, and reduces damaging cholesterol, this discipline is still rejected by a majority of Americans. Instead of doing the recommended thirty to sixty minutes of exercise on most days of the week, many of us fondly dream of a new one-a-day pill that would reduce our weight, strengthen our hearts and other muscles, and increase blood flow to our brains.

An obvious corollary exists between physical exercise and spiritual exercise. Many of us long for a one-a-day reform pill that would save us from having to engage in the hard discipline of daily conversion. We can long to be vaccinated—as with a flu shot—against various sin viruses and our unruly inner beasts, such as the ones Jesus encountered in his lenten desert experience. Aren't there some painless substitutions for the hard work of exercising and taming our inner demons? Sorry, TINA: "There Is No Alternative," as former British

Prime Minister Margaret Thatcher would say. However, before whipping your demons into shape, do not confuse *exercising* your demons with *exorcising* them.

Lent's twin focal points include a preparation for baptism and a renewal course in how to live our lifelong baptismal reformation. During Lent, everyone is a convert. The preparation for and living of our baptismal calling require conversion—changing what is negative and destructive into what is positive and productive. Exercise is critical to this conversion process, just as it is in the taming of wild horses or lions. They are tamed and trained by repetitive exercises and reinforced by reward and punishment. It is the same when converting our dark energies into positive powers of life.

For example, lust is the vice among the seven capital sins that today usually means excessive, uncontrolled sexual craving. However, lust was once used in a positive sense for being vigorously, passionately excited about art or music or anything else. Converting lust means exercising and taming the selfish desires out of that life-energy, and changing it into a powerful tool for loving and caring for others, into a tool for justice, and even into a tool for prayer and holiness.

Look back over your list of pet faults and you will find an index of potential converts. Instead of casting them into the lenten garbage can, employ the patient discipline of exercising again and again their positive qualities and you will convert them into powerful allies for your holiness.

THE SECOND WEEK OF LENT

Friday of the Second Week in Lent

There's a threadbare story about an old Vermont farmer who, when asked if he believed in original sin, answered, "Believe in it? I've seen it!" Even a glance at our global reality reveals evidence of the unbelievable evil that humans inflict on one another. The old farmer said he'd seen it and so have we: the diabolical evils of war, racial and religious violence, exploitation of the poor, and the neglect of the homeless and hungry by the wealthy and comfortable, just to name a few.

Giving alms and caring for the poor are among the traditional works of Lent and need to be at the heart of our ongoing religious disciplines. Lent should be a time for an audit of our financial books—a time to be evaluated on how well we have administered the monies entrusted to our care by God. While we may think that all the money we've earned is our personal property, that's not the fiscal ethic of the gospels where Jesus says, "From everyone to whom much has been given, much will be required" (Lk 12:48).

Are you financially healthy? Are you a generous sharer of your wealth with those who are in need? Does your care of the poor reflect the norm of generosity in the United States? Many of us think of America as being the most generous nation in terms of feeding the starving and giving aid to the poor countries of the world. In reality, however, while being the richest country, America ranks *last* among the top twenty developed nations in donating to the poor and sick of the world! Allow that shocking fact to challenge you to examine the depth of your generosity in response to your solemn duty to feed the poor, cloth the naked, and give shelter to the homeless (see Mt 25:37–38).

Besides almsgiving and caring for the poor, another traditional work of Lent is fasting. At various times in history, this ascetic practice was taken to radical extremes. Some ascetics would fast to the point of near starvation, something no responsible person today would praise or encourage. Paradoxically, spiritual fasting to the edge of starvation can help to cure our sins. A story will help to explain this:

Once, an old Cherokee told his grandson about the great fight going on inside of him. It was a conflict between two wolves. One wolf was his urge to anger, envy, greed, arrogance, self-pity, revenge, false pride, and resentment. The other wolf, the old man said, was his inclination to live in joy, peace, hope, and love, to be generous, humble, compassionate, and trusting of all humankind. When he was finished, the grandson asked, "Which wolf wins, grandfather?" His reply was simply, "The one I feed."

Which of your wolves is winning? Perhaps it's time to starve one. . . .

THE SECOND WEEK OF LENT

SATURDAY OF
THE SECOND
WEEK IN LENT

A wise man once defined god as whatever was the most important thing in one's life. Using this definition makes it obvious that we are surrounded by the worship of gods with names like Business Success, Professional Advancement, Making Money, Social Acceptance, Sex, Security, Alcohol, Drugs, Beauty, Automobiles, Expensive Homes, and all of our other favorite idols.

Regardless of their names, all idols require human sacrifices. Consider the hundreds of thousands of human sacrifices on the altars of those glitzy gods who are worshiped in corporate skyscraper temples and in the arenas of athletics and show business. Private homes also have their idol shrines where the humdrum domestic gods of Cleanliness, Order, Efficiency, and the deity of Having-My-Way are frequently worshiped. Mirrors are shrines of idolatry to the gods of the Ego and Perpetual Youthfulness, before whom we spend much time in personal grooming and beautifying. In the worship of these gods, we sacrifice hours exercising and undergoing the pains of dieting..

Last Saturday, we reflected about creating Sunday-*Sabbat* days of leisure from work. There is a connection between that commandment and the first commandment forbidding the worship of idols. Most of us believe that with the exception of a few remote places deep in dark jungles, idol worship disappeared centuries ago; but in fact, idol worship today is healthy, thriving, and even practiced by devout Christians. Many churches worship the idols of material wealth and institutional power right alongside their worship of God. Whenever only precise adherence to every minuscule rubric makes worship authentic or whenever earthly abundance is lauded as reward for Christian discipleship, there are idols in the sanctuary. The Bible becomes an idol whenever it becomes the unquestioned, absolute authority, particularly when it is applied to a current situation without considering the original context in which the biblical text was written. Church disciplines and moral dictates become idols when they eclipse the one, true, loving, and compassionate God.

This Saturday's gospel reading of the prodigal son relates the story of a father and his unconditional acceptance of his wayward, sinful son. Jesus' parable is a medicinal story, intending to heal the hearts of the Pharisees and scribes who were outraged because Jesus was violating their religious codes by welcoming sinners as companions and eating with them. The paradox is that these righteous, devout Jews would rather have embraced bloody martyrdom than worship a foreign god, yet they had made gods out of their religious human-made laws.

Let us not judge but be compassionate toward those unfortunate pious Pharisees and religious lawyers, for you and I sin just as easily as did they whenever we make idols out of our religious, cultural, or personal rituals and laws.

THE SECOND WEEK OF LENT

THE THIRD
WEEK
OF LENT

THIRD SUNDAY
IN LENT

Jesus opens a can of worms today! That familiar saying refers to any inextricable tangle of problems that is released as soon as an issue is addressed. The can is opened when Jesus encounters the caretakers of God's Temple in Jerusalem, which bore a large label: Don't Tamper With Our Religion! What most people saw as an acceptable or perhaps even praiseworthy use of that sacred space, he finds repulsive and diseased and, therefore, purges it (Jn 2:13–25). Earlier prophets had likewise condemned the Temple's empty-hearted yet rubrically precise sacrificial worship, but today the Galilean Prophet's daring act opens a can of worms.

Worms, in the form of leeches, were once considered the great cure-all for whatever made one sick. These three-to four-inch-long bloodsuckers were gathered from swamps for medicinal purposes. With their sharp teeth, they would open an incision in the flesh and then suck out a patient's blood. The prescription for headaches was to place six large leeches on the forehead for several hours. For depression, they were used three to five times a day, so they would draw at least two pints of blood; hysterical patients were drained of four pints or until they became calm. As strange as all this may sound, the use of leeches was actually a medical advance over the customary practice that began in 400 B.C. by the Greeks, who instead drew blood with a knife to purge the body. We still have relics of this cure: the red-and-white striped poles in front of barbershops. In medieval times these were also bleeders. Indeed, bleeding was a commonplace prophylactic protection against various afflictions. It was even used religiously to ensure chastity when older monks would bleed young monks to reduce their passionate urges.

Was idolatry the temple disease that Jesus sought to heal by drawing blood with his whip? In this Sunday's Exodus reading (Ex 20:1–3, 7–8, 12–17), God thunders out against the disease of idol worship: "You shall not have other gods before me. You shall not bow down to them or worship them." The precise priestly rituals for Temple sacrifice in the time of Jesus required the use of only perfect animals, which led to the profitable business of providing these to poor pilgrims. Besides leading to frequent abuse and exploitation of the needy, Jesus found these practices idolatrous. To what extent do we today bow down before religious laws and customs as if they were gods?

Take a cue from today's story of Jesus purging God's house of prayer and examine the health of your personal temple. To purge your prayer life of the disease *templeitis* neither leeches nor the bleeder's knife is required but only a heartfelt resolution. Like the flu virus, *templeitis* constantly mutates into new strains that resist treatment. A fruitful Lent and a healthy spiritual life require continuous purging of our own bodily house of prayer. You might take Louis XIII of France, who had himself bled twice a day, except on holy days, as a patron for this ongoing purging and transformation of your prayer life.

THE THIRD WEEK OF LENT

MONDAY OF
THE THIRD
WEEK IN LENT

Doctor Jesus sought to heal the strain of *templeitis* that leads to perhaps the most forgotten of the seven deadly sins. Among the seven: pride, envy, anger, melancholy, acedia, greed, gluttony, and lust, it would be as rare as a blue moon to confess to the sin stuck in the middle, acedia. True to Jesus' prediction that the last shall become first, last place lust and its trail of sexual sins now usually rank first among the openly recognized affronts to moral values. Acedia, on the other hand, is usually regarded with relative indifference, which is probably appropriate since this deadly sin manifests itself in symptoms of spiritual apathy. This strain of *templeitis* is also expressed as dryness in prayer, boredom at worship, and the itch to check the time while meditating and praying.

Another symptom of acedia is listlessness at worship which easily infects its leaders. This spiritual illness creates clerical robots that listlessly mouth the liturgy. Church choirs infected with it may sing on key, but they are more concerned about performing well than praying. Acedia is also contagious. It quickly spreads beyond our prayers and worship into our living prayer of social justice. The famous silent majority typically suffers from the inertia of acedia—remaining silent and sedentary against local, national, and church-related injustices. Among the crippling effects of this oft-overlooked sin of acedia is a spiritual lethargy that leaves many of us complacent about hollow, poorly planned and celebrated liturgies that cannot nourish or inspire. When church attendance is valued more than compassion and when rubrics are more important than prayer or devotion, Jesus echoes the prophet Hosea, "For I desire steadfast love and not sacrifice, the knowledge of God rather than burnt offerings" (Hos 6:6).

The Pharmacist of Nazareth's cure for acedia was to mix all Ten Commandments together in his bowl and then use his pestle to grind them into a single one: "You shall love the Lord your God with all your heart, and with all your soul, and with all your strength, and with all your mind; and your neighbor as yourself" (Lk 10:27). To create the wellness of authentic prayer and the necessary medicine for wholesome life, Jesus produced a miracle drug: a love of God, of oneself, and all of life that is wholehearted, whole-souled, whole-minded, and whole-bodied.

To heal hard-to-detect-but-deadly acedia, we need to take Jesus' medicine of wholehearted love daily. We also need to remember that it's a big pill to swallow! Doing everything we do with all our heart requires dedication, especially when it comes to praying. It might not be possible to recite multiple prayers several times a day with the heartfelt intensity prescribed by Pharmacist Jesus. So experiment: pray less, even just a single sentence, so that you can fill every word of prayer with all your heart, soul, and mind. God prefers quality to quantity—always.

THE THIRD WEEK OF LENT

TUESDAY OF THE THIRD WEEK IN LENT

Does Jesus exaggerate? Can we take him seriously in today's gospel when he says we must forgive seventy-seven times—an infinite number of times (Mt 18:21–35)? Does Nazareth's physician use such exaggeration because some medicines are effective only in large doses? Certainly, a more powerful or larger dose of medication is required for the deadly illness of tightly clutching our anger and resentment when we are injured or betrayed. The very emotions that prevent us from forgiving another person who has caused us pain create additional pain in us! An inability or unwillingness to forgive creates high blood pressure, which can lead to heart disease, stroke, and many other illnesses. On the other hand, forgiving others actually reduces blood pressure and elevates our sense of wellness.

While Jesus prescribed forgiveness, he didn't describe how we are to practice that good medicine. Yet, a few suggestions might be helpful. Begin with fully acknowledging the painful wound of being betrayed at the hands of a friend, lover, or spouse. All wounds hurt and require treatment, but the first step to well-being is to acknowledge the pain, not to merely bandage the wound by denying the agony it brings. Second, we might attempt to understand the reasons why the individual acted as she or he did. Third, we can review our options:

- We can choose to be a passive victim, pretending the offense didn't happen.
- We can become the wounded aggressor and seek revenge.
- We determine to end the relationship.
- We can begin the process of forgiving the offender.

This last choice, to start a process of healing reconciliation, is done not just for the benefit of the offender, but mainly for our own welfare and wellness.

Jesus the Physician knew that forgiveness is an ongoing process and so he prescribed that we forgive seventy-seven times. If we are fortunate and our wound is not terribly severe, a conscious act of forgiveness once an hour for seven hours, or even once a day for a week, may heal our injured heart. If, however, our wound is as wide and deep as the Amazon, full recovery may take seventy-seven days of pardoning.

Whether your pardoning therapy is brief or lengthy, engage in that process with a sense of high honor, knowing that by your forgiving you are becoming godlike. Be extraordinarily grateful that in this pardoning process you will experience a twofold healing of soul and body. The hidden blessing in your generous and unconditional forgiveness is that God is simultaneously granting you unconditional pardon seventy-seven times for your sins. Jesus has indeed given to us a truly miraculous medicine.

THE THIRD WEEK OF LENT

Rᵀ

WEDNESDAY OF THE THIRD WEEK IN LENT

D r. Albert Schweitzer was fond of saying, "Each person has a wise physician within them." Today, think about making an appointment with your inner physician. This reminds me of a cartoon I saw recently. The drawing shows a man standing at a receptionist's desk; the woman seated behind it says to him, "Yes, your appointment to see Dr. Murphy is at 1:00 this afternoon, and Dr. Murphy's appointment to see you is at 2:30."

A recent survey taken by the American College of Emergency Physicians found that the average time spent waiting in an emergency room is 6.2 hours. Patients with incomes of less than $20,000 a year waited for treatment for a whopping average of 13.3 hours! Whether it's an emergency or a scheduled appointment, waiting to see a physician is something we've come to expect in this country.

Besides being expected, perhaps this waiting is also intentional. I've often wondered if a secret part of the famous Hippocratic oath taken by physicians is, "Thou shalt make thy patients wait for long periods of time, for in this useless idleness healing happens." Flipping through old magazines or watching your fingernails grow in a doctor's reception room hardly seems medicinal, yet it may actually be essential to healing. Being forced to remain in a suspended state of non-activity could help to cure the sin at the top of the original hit parade of sins—pride. Important people do not have to wait for anything. Having to wait our turn reminds us that there are others who also have aliments, perhaps afflictions far more serious than our own. Waiting thus reminds us of the needs of others. The forced leisure of a waiting room or an airport can purge us of the frenzied hyperactivity of contemporary life. In America today, one out of three people suffers from hypertension, a number which is up from one out of four only ten years ago!

Frederick the Great of Prussia, a vigorous man in every situation he faced, would order the royal physician, right in the midst of a fierce battle, to cut open a vein and bleed him to restore his calm. Recall this calm-restoring method of Frederick the Wise when you experience highly charged situations at work or at home and find ways to bleed yourself of unhealthy hypertension. You might, for example, take a few moments for deep breathing, focusing your attention on each breath to help you purge boiling emotions and restore your inner peace.

Schweitzer's interior physician is the Holy Healing Spirit, who, if you wait patiently in silent stillness, will reveal your hidden ailments of body, mind, and soul—and their cures.

THE THIRD WEEK OF LENT

Thursday of
the Third
Week in Lent

Theologian Anthony Padovano said, "It is not healthy to live and work in one world and to believe and pray in another. The harmony of these two worlds is an issue in the development of a contemporary spirituality." While it is common to blame our contemporary secular culture for this unhealthy division of praying in one world while living in another, it is, in reality, an ancient malady.

Jesus, the Teacher-Physician from Nazareth, proposed the cure of living an integrated life—residing and worshiping in one world. As a sacred surgeon, he fused the two separate worlds of temple worship and daily life by revealing how ordinary everyday activities like eating meals, attending weddings, and extending hospitality toward strangers are actually be holy events. Religions sometimes draw distinct boundary lines that separate the ordinary from the sacred by establishing certain places, people, and days as holy and determining the rest to be profane—literately "outside the *fanum*," outside the temple. Jesus turned over the religious apple cart by making the profane into the sacred, as all the redemptive actions of his life were done outside the temple in the profane hustle and bustle of ordinary life.

As a teacher, Jesus demonstrated how loving, caring interactions with others are sacred rituals that are as holy as any sacrifices performed by priests in the temple. His teaching is echoed in the second chapter of 1 Peter, "Let yourselves be a holy priesthood to offer spiritual sacrifices acceptable to God . . . " (1 Pet 2:5). Paul agrees: "Present your bodies as a living sacrifice, holy and acceptable to God, which is your spiritual worship" (Rom 12:1). This bit of wisdom could be rephrased, "Make your bodily actions of walking, working, loving, and caring into sacrifices that are holy and pleasing to God."

Lent provides us opportunities to sharpen our skills. Everyday things in which each work of our hands—whether fixing supper or folded in prayer—can be offered as sacrifices pleasing to God. To live and sleep in such a seamlessly holy world requires no theological tricks or mystical maneuvers; only living as Jesus did. His entire life was a seamless act of worship, since he experienced the Divine Mystery abiding within himself and made God present wherever he was. Jesus transformed every place into a temple sanctuary. His greatest wish was that you and I would also share his holy intimacy— as he prayed, "As you, Father, are in me and I am in you, may they also be in us . . . so that they may be one, as we are one" (Jn 17:21–22). This awesome divine indwelling wasn't unique to him, or he wouldn't have longed for his disciples to become just as conscious of this divine union as he was. Let this lenten Thursday inspire you to strive to make your life a priestly, living sacrifice pleasing to God.

THE THIRD WEEK OF LENT

Friday of the Third Week in Lent

Good Friday is only three weeks from today, which makes this a good time to reflect on those powerful words in the Lord's Prayer, "Forgive us our sins." The reality of the Lord's Passion should prevent us from ever reciting these words absentmindedly. Whether we use the words "trespasses," "debts" or "sins," they are hardly idle or simply pious words, for Jesus promised that whatever we ask for in prayer we would receive! Devoutly petitioning God to forgive our sins implies that we expect God to grant us absolution, which in turn implies a need for pardon. On this lenten Friday, take time to examine your life for sin and as you reflect on your faults, major or minor, don't overlook the sin of sodomy!

Before slamming this book shut in disgust at such a horrifying suggestion, reflect on the words of Ezekiel about Jerusalem: "This was the guilt of your sister Sodom: she and her daughters had pride, excess of food, and prosperous ease, but did not aid the poor and needy" (Ez 16:49). Here Ezekiel declares that Sodom's real sin is the complacent neglect of the needy and poor! Nowhere in scripture does it say that homosexuality caused God to destroy Sodom, yet long centuries of religious prejudice have earmarked this as the cause of its destruction. Even though sodomy became the legal criminal term for sexual acts judged to be abnormal, Jesus linked the punishment of Sodom with its failure to offer hospitality (see Mt 10:11–15). And Ezekiel directly connected the wickedness of Sodom with its overfed, complacent ignoring of the needs of the poor.

Scrutinize your behavior today for any sins of complacent sodomy: the failure to reach out to feed the hungry, to provide hospitality to the homeless, to bring comfort to the unemployed or assistance to those in need. Ezekiel's use of the term "complacent" should sting us faithful church-attending Christians as painfully as the suggestion of being judged as sodomites are! Complacent Christians settled in their comfortable prosperity are smug, self-satisfied, and self-righteous in their belief that Bible reading and church attendance fulfills their moral obligations. Being self-satisfied, they are self-blinded to the truth that God desires *mercy* toward others—tender loving care—as our most authentic form of worship.

Last Friday's reflection dealt with our national complacency as a so-called "Christian" nation that places last among the world's twenty richest nations in providing relief to the poor and sick of the world. You may be powerless to change this shameful national neglect or the other exploitative policies of the United States, but you can change yourself! The next time, before you pray the Lord's Prayer to ask that your sins be forgiven, take a moment to examine yourself for the sins of sodomy and complacency.

THE THIRD WEEK OF LENT

SATURDAY OF THE THIRD WEEK IN LENT

At the end of this third week of lenten discipline and inner reflection, we look forward to Restaurant Sunday—a term derived from the practice of medicinal purging. After the demise of the medical practice of bloodletting, the use of enemas for cleansing and restoring vitality and sexual vigor became a European health fad in the 1800s. In those years, popular enemas that were used to restore sexual powers were called *restaurants,* from the French "to restore."

Constantly working and keeping incessantly busy can cause us to become emotionally and spiritually constipated. After a long week of work, relieve yourself with a Restaurant Sunday. Being purged of a week's worth of toil, it is a good day for *idle* worship, instead of the worship of *idols.* Worship means "to reverence, love, or respect," and, oh, how we need to respect the powers of being idle! The Latin word for leisure is *otium,* and the absence of leisure is *negotium,* which is translated as "business," "work," or "trouble." And the trouble with our culture's work-driven lifestyle is that it blocks the flow of life.

A good prescription to heal this blockage is the laxative of play, that delightful activity of leisure time. Play is an essential activity at every stage of human life. As we age and move from one stage of life to another, the ways we play also change. Yet that activity, which we usually think of as merely a childhood occupation, remains indispensable throughout life. Indeed, play is the form of prayer and worship that is most pleasing to God on Restaurant Sundays.

Play implies having fun, amusing ourselves alone or with others. Play with others is a form of communal worship and communal healing. While a popular Sunday afternoon entertainment is watching others play sports on television, this doesn't have the same effect as actually playing. Since play is a childlike activity, adults often feel guilty about playing unless it is in some recognizable form of adult recreation. We see life as serious business, especially the spiritual life, and so those seeking holiness usually don't want to squander their time playing or amusing themselves. Indeed, this may be one reason for all those unhappy, constipated-looking faces seen on the statues of saints! If your life lacks frequent playtime, Restaurant Sunday is a good day to change that by making play as important as physical exercise or a healthy diet. You'll be delighted at the cleansing, restorative results!

THE THIRD WEEK OF LENT

THE FOURTH
WEEK
OF LENT

FOURTH SUNDAY IN LENT

A United Press release told the story of a hospital in a Midwestern city where officials had discovered that its fire-fighting equipment had never been connected to the city's water main. For thirty-five years the patients and medical staff had felt safe at the sight of those brightly polished brass valves and outlets placed throughout the hospital. Yet the security of all this expert fire-fighting technology was an illusion, for all of it was connected to an underground pipe that extended only four feet from the hospital before it stopped!

Most Christians feel just such surety at the sight of a cross—never questioning its effectiveness. The issue for us isn't whether images of the cross are connected to the source, but rather how we are connected to the cross! Are we linked to the cross only remotely, as a symbol that no longer speaks to us, or are we intimately united with it? During Lent, churches frequently put up large, rugged wooden crosses draped with purple cloths. The Roman cross, which was once a shockingly hideous image, can easily become impotent today, unable to move those who see it to greater zeal,

THE FOURTH WEEK OF LENT

heroism, or prayer. Perhaps our lenten cross would be radically enlivened if, rather than using a long purple cloth, we draped it instead with a serpent!

In today's gospel (Jn 3:14–21), Jesus is compared to such a serpent intertwined on the cross. This shocking image comes from the time when the Israelites were complaining about their difficulties in the desert after their exodus from Egypt and were punished by a plague of poisonous serpents. They pleaded to Moses for help and God instructed him to make a serpent out of bronze and to place it on a pole. Any who were bitten and looked upon it were healed. The author of John compares the healing salvation brought by Jesus being lifted up on the cross to the bronze serpent of Moses and his people in the desert.

The cross of Christ is a boundless source of healing if you are connected to it. This symbol of suffering is transformed in either the form of the *Tau* cross, which prophetically symbolizes that we now live in the reign of God, or the cross of Calvary by which Christ overcame death itself. Have you ever had a personal experience of being liberated or healed from some paralyzing illness or addiction and then realized that your healing was connected with the cross in your room or home? Consider the practice of consciously uniting your suffering, whether it stems from the crippling pains of arthritis or a throbbing migraine headache, to the source of healing— the cross. One simple ritual would be to touch your fingers to your cross and pray that uniting your pains with those of Christ will be a redemptive Holy Communion.

The Fourth Week of Lent

MONDAY OF THE FOURTH WEEK IN LENT

Those sick Hebrews wandering in the desert had lived in Egypt and so would have recognized Moses' serpent on a staff as a symbol of the healing god, Aesculapius. The staff of the Greek god of medicine was intertwined with a serpent and was recognizable throughout the Mediterranean world. Since ancient times, the sick had come on pilgrimage to be cured in his temple at Epidaurus. While the temple healing ceremony involved rest and a ritual cleansing of the body, the most important part of the ritual would send shudders down your spine. Those who wanted to be healed had to sleep overnight on the floor of Aesculapius's temple, which was covered with countless crawling serpents that were sacred to the god! Today in the ruins of this temple you can still find numerous marble plaques of tribute inscribed with the name of patients grateful for the miraculous cures that they received at his shrine.

The single coiled serpent on the staff of Aesculapius, whose name means "forever gentle," is an emblem of the medical profession and is the basis for the more recognizable caduceus, which has two serpents, entwined on a staff crowned by a pair of wings. This caduceus is actually the staff of Hermes, the messenger of the gods (or Mercury, as the Romans called him). Surprisingly, though, he was not the god of healing. Hermes, or Mercury, was the god who oversaw business, profit, and cunning theft. He was also the god who conducted the dead to the underworld. The widespread belief in the healing powers of serpents may help to explain the confusion over why Hermes's staff rather than Aesculapius's was chosen to represent the art and science of medicine.

In this Monday's lenten gospel (Jn 4:43–54), a royal official approaches the forever gentle Jesus—the new Aesculapius—and begs him to come and heal his son, who is suffering from a deadly fever. Jesus sends the official home, telling him that his son is well. The official puts his trust in what Jesus says and departs. His servants meet him on his way home with the good news that the fever has left his son! When the official asks them what time the healing happened, he discovers that it was at the precise moment when he trusted in what Jesus had said to him. Faith—or, better, trust—moves mountains and heals.

The springtime of Lent is a season to grow in great trust, in the kind of confident expectation that the royal official placed in the words of Jesus. On the cross, even though it seemed that God had abandoned him, Jesus clung to God during those last painful hours of his death. Pray today for an increased trust in God and in the promises of God that Jesus passed on to us. Make a distinction in your prayer between faith as belief in dogmas and doctrinal issues and trust, which implies a personal relationship of confident reliance and assurance. Realize that only an intimate, loving relationship births the resilient hope-saturated qualities of trust.

THE FOURTH WEEK OF LENT

TUESDAY OF
THE FOURTH
WEEK IN LENT

God instructed Moses to make an image of the bronze serpent, an act that violated the First, and primal Commandment forbidding the making of idols! In today's gospel (Jn 5:1–16), Jesus violates the Third Commandment by healing a paralyzed man on the Sabbath. These "transgressions" that are done for the sake of healing give us insight into the message of this lenten Tuesday.

Before healing the lame man, Jesus, as a good physician, asks the man who has been paralyzed for thirty-eight years, "Do you want to be healed?" That may sound like a stupid question, but it's not, for some who are sick do not really want to be healed! Indeed, that same critical question is asked of each of us. Lent is the season for sinners, not saints, a holy time for healing the sick, not the healthy. Jesus the Healer spoke plainly when he said that he had come to heal the sick and not those who had no need of a physician. If, indeed, you are sick, do you want to be healed? Do you really want to be different than you are today? Over the years, we become attached to our emotional, behavioral, and psychological afflictions. Not only do we grow accustomed to them; we sometimes even like them. Worn down at the heels is the expression, "This is who I am: Love me or leave me! I don't plan on changing at my age."

When doing our self-examination, we might become aware of a common disease with a Latin medical name borrowed from the Roman poet Virgil: *Latet anguis in herbe,* "a snake lurks in the grass." This expression refers to having a hidden enemy, but in a poignant play on words it also points to the popular affliction of having "a snake in the glass"—the looking glass! Our unrecognized afflictions paralyze us precisely because we are blind to their existence. So, today's prescription is to go and look mindfully in the mirror.

While our religious and social institutions are badly in need of healing, we can only heal the world by healing ourselves first. Looking at yourself in the mirror, besides the signs of aging, do you see anything disturbing? Peer deeply beneath the surface of your skin and probe your belief system: Do you believe violence is necessary to maintain order, or that the poor are lazy, or that the rich are greedy? Scrutinize your personal biases, your array of prejudices (whether good or bad), your preconceived notions about people, religion, politics, or life.

After this examination of your internal health, ask yourself the same question that Jesus asked that cripple: "Do you want to be healed?" Don't be in any hurry to answer. Take time to ponder carefully if you are truly interested in a healing that isn't a quick fix, an instantaneous cure, like that of the paralyzed man in the gospel story. If you do wish to be healed, be forewarned that the Galilean Healer may prescribe surgery for you. You may have to undergo the knife, a sacred scalpel that only you can use.

THE FOURTH WEEK OF LENT

WEDNESDAY OF THE FOURTH WEEK IN LENT

Mirror inspection can reveal—to those with eyes to see—a basic prejudice that is perhaps one of the most crippling of diseases. This prejudice is a negative, invalid judgment about you! All prejudice is evil. It sinfully rejects or degrades the uniquely beautiful person made in the image of goodness, which is author Peter Gomes's expression for the image of God. This self-prejudice has been called self-loathing; we bemoan ourselves as inferior to others because this or that physical or natural quality is lacking.

This disease first appeared long ago in the East, when worm-infected fruit in the Garden of Eden carried its virus. Since then, it has become a worldwide pandemic leaping from generation to generation. Theologians call this pestilence "original sin," and the great spiritual writer Henri Nouwen diagnosed this disease as "humanity's endless capacity for self-rejection."

Psychologists agree that a prime source of bigotry, intolerance, and disdain toward others is our self-loathing. The stronger the self-prejudice, the greater is the need to treat some particular class, race, or group of persons as inferior to ourselves. History has produced many erroneous cures for this affliction of inadequacy, like greed and power. The rich and powerful are admired because of their wealth and puffed-up positions of prestige. Yet, while some may be fooled by wealth or power, the mirror on your wall is not deceived!

The first symptom of the original disease was an awareness of one's own nakedness. When Adam and Eve realized that they were naked, they were ashamed. Self-prejudice produces the embarrassment of nakedness even when we are fully clothed. We suffer this shame when we feel the lack of some quality of body or mind that makes us feel inferior. The old home remedy for this pain is to cover our inner nakedness with an expensive sports car, some important profession or office, a large, lavish home, closets full of clothing in the latest styles, or having children whose successes mirror pride back to us as parents.

However, Jesus the Galilean Healer prescribed the most effective, guaranteed, and reliable cure with his healing commandment, "Love God and your neighbor as yourself." But we must live this commandment backwards. With all our heart and soul we must love ourselves as we were created, with all our deficiencies and imperfections. Those of us wounded by self-prejudice often have to start here, or else we'll never be able to love our faulty neighbor. Only by an unprejudiced love for our self will we be able to love our God, who lovingly designed each of us as precious in the divine image.

Good self-esteem produces good health by helping us to develop a powerful immune system against viruses that target both spirit and mind. An affirmative self-mage engenders resilience to cope with the difficult challenges of life, and it ensures rapid regeneration after daily defeats and disappointments. So, during these last days of our

THE FOURTH WEEK OF LENT

Pharmaceutical Lent, diligently follow Jesus' prescription for dealing with the disease of self-loathing.

THE FOURTH WEEK OF LENT

THURSDAY OF THE FOURTH WEEK IN LENT

Chiropractic healing seems required for those suffering in today's first reading (Ex 32:1–14). With disgust, God points out the affliction of those people whom Moses has led out of Egypt to freedom: "I have seen this people, how stiff-necked they are" (Ex 32:9). Paradoxically, the problem of being stiff-necked requires more the treatment of an ophthalmologist, an eye doctor, than that of a chiropractor or physical therapist. The inability to lower one's head in a gesture of humility is often caused by self-blindness. Those so afflicted lack honest mirror-vision and so cannot see their own faults or sins but, instead, often view themselves as righteously justified and pleasing to God.

In the Gospel of John the woman caught in adultery is about to be stoned by the scribes and Pharisees when Jesus sends them back to look in their mirrors by saying, "Let anyone among you who is without sin be the first to throw a stone at her" (Jn 8:7). Those who are humble have the capacity to be compassionate since they know how easily they have personally failed to love God perfectly. The Sufi mystic Rumi says, "Your doctor must have a broken leg to doctor."

Indeed, our broken legs and broken hearts make us good doctors to those suffering the various afflictions of being human.

Compassion is the prime requirement in any wellness regimen for all of us who are inflexible in our principles and doctrines. This neck stiffness creates tunnel vision, the inability to see other sides of a situation. Conformist Christians often manifest religious rigidity that reveals a fear of falling into sin if they don't have the security of high, rigid fences to hide behind. Their personal need to protect themselves with unyielding moral or ritual disciplines is projected outward as a necessary requirement for everyone else. When you encounter those suffering from this sickness, be compassionate.

While many people prefer to whisper their sins in the darkness of a confessional, the mystic Rumi offers a twofold healing wisdom: "Your defects are the ways that glory is manifested." And, "There is nothing worse than thinking you are well enough." That double dose of medicine begins first by allowing God to be glorified by our defects and weaknesses, since with grace we can accomplish good deeds that give glory to God. Rumi's second piece of healing wisdom is that while rejecting negative self-prejudice by embracing with love all of who we are, we also need to be careful not to fall into the insidious trap of thinking that we are well and so have no need of healing.

THE FOURTH WEEK OF LENT

Friday of the Fourth Week in Lent

"**L**et us condemn him to a shameful death." These words from today's first reading (Wis 2:1a, 12–22) foreshadow the reality of Good Friday. Our Friday reflection continues this week's theme of snakes—perhaps the most feared, if not despised, of all of God's creatures. Our imbedded prejudice against them, even when they are not poisonous, can make it extremely difficult to associate healing with serpents.

Yet fright at the sight of a snake isn't natural. Upon finding a snake, a small toddler will often innocently pick it up and try to play with it. As with all of our prejudices and hatreds, our fear of snakes is a learned behavior. And, indeed, we hate what we fear! The cures at the shrine of Aesculapius are especially fascinating because the patients had to sleep overnight in his temple while his sacred snakes slithered around and over them. Were their healings somehow connected to the fact that they intimately had to encounter that which they so greatly feared? How those patients were liberated from their fears should inspire us to seek similar healings this Lent.

Prejudicial hatred of anyone is a sinful abomination to God, who created every person in the image of goodness and beauty. Our society is rightfully proud of its recent successes at rising above much of its racial, ethnic, and religious prejudices. However, one prejudice remains that is actually seen by some as good and godly—the prejudice against homosexuals. We need to remember that God creates gays and lesbians, just as God creates all of us and that sexual attraction is not a chosen characteristic. Negative references to homosexuality in the Bible are as outdated as its affirmation in places of human slavery and polygamy. Jesus never condemned homosexuality or even mentioned it. Yet, even for those who continue to judge it as sinful, that belief does not grant religious license to have anti gay prejudices and to malign gays any more than those guilty of another sin.

Just as our fear of snakes creates an intense hatred toward them, our fear of those who act differently, look differently, or love differently than the majority creates a repulsion toward them. "Let us condemn him to a shameful death" was the hate-filled verdict cast upon Jesus. Let us not cast this same verdict upon any of our fellow human beings just because we fear or cannot accept who they are.

THE FOURTH WEEK OF LENT

SATURDAY OF THE FOURTH WEEK IN LENT

"**L**enten Molting Days" would be a good name for the coming week. For the past four weeks we've been involved in becoming new persons and it's time to shed the old self. Serpents are good role models for disciples of Jesus who are called to ongoing reformation and transformation. Several times a year, snakes grow completely new skins and shed their old ones in a process called molting. The old skin is removed as the snake rubs itself between two rocks or along rough branches of a bush. Then the snake slips out of its old skin, leaving it behind turned inside out but perfectly intact, like a hollow tube. So whenever you find yourself between a rock and a hard place, rejoice, because it might just be the place to complete your lenten healing!

Snakes do not have to struggle painfully to shake off their old skins. When the time is right they just slip out of them and leave them behind. The same should be true for us. For even if we have earnestly disciplined ourselves over the past weeks, these next days might not be the right time for us to shed our old selves. So, don't force it. Jesus, forever gentle in his healing, never called his disciples to violent reform. His pattern was first to invite those wishing to be his students to come, learn of him, and imitate his selfless loving. He understood the spiritual rule of ripening—that in the process of maturing in the spirit, our sinful habits, attitudes, or behavior will fall away as naturally as the old skin of a snake.

Truly, the dilemma of finding oneself between a rock and a hard place can become the occasion to take the last step of transformation, but we need to do so mindful that it is not the final step. The reformation of discipleship is a *lifelong* process of skin shedding. In fact, the closer we come to the Light, the more we see in ourselves what must be purged and left behind if we are to be fully filled with the Light. As inner darkness lessens, we can see more clearly even the slightest spiritual imperfections that now cry out to be removed. So, blessed are those who, serpent-like, shed their skin not once but continuously.

It's not easy to have snakes as models for Christian discipleship because of our biblical prejudice against them as a primal source of evil and an image of Satan that must be crushed. If you have difficulty thinking of serpents as holy symbols, recall what the Master said when he sent his disciples out into the world, "Be wise as serpents and innocent as doves" (Mt 10:16). So, be as clever as a serpent and let your next rock-and-a-hard-place provide you with an opportunity for fresh and glorious renewal.

THE FOURTH WEEK OF LENT

The Fifth Week of Lent

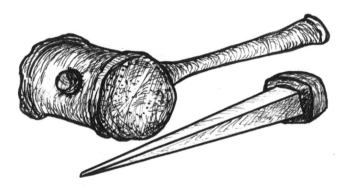

FIFTH SUNDAY IN LENT

"**N**ow my soul is troubled," Jesus laments in the gospel of this Sunday before Palm Sunday (Jn 12:20–33). "And what should I say: Father, save me from this hour?" His head must have ached from the pounding of conflicting thoughts—on the one hand, embracing whatever God and his destiny required and, on the other hand, his natural self-preservation that urged him to save himself. As a patient in this agony, Jesus may have felt like the woman whose doctor asked her, "Where does it hurt?" Looking up at him with a grimace, she answered, "Oh doctor, where doesn't it hurt?" Plato taught that physical pain is also experienced by the soul. Those who experience intense pain know that their souls ache as much as their bodies do.

In Gethsemane, anticipating his tortuous death on the cross, Jesus endured an all-encompassing suffering: his sweat became like drops of blood as he cried out, "I am deeply grieved, even to death" (Mk 14:34). Once pain has reached a certain threshold, it expands beyond the site of its origin, causing an avalanche of biochemical reactions that affect the circulation, muscles, tissues, and organs of the body—as anyone who suffers the excruciating pain of a migraine headache can affirm.

Suffering from headaches seems to be a problem that has existed since the dawn of humanity. Eight thousand years ago, Sumerian pharmacists offered relief from headaches with the medicine of pulverized bark of a willow tree. In medieval times, medicinal blood-sucking leeches were applied to the forehead. In the mid-sixteenth century, if a court official of Russian Tsar Ivan the Terrible complained of a headache, the tsar would order nails to be driven into his head. Although this cure sounds more like a diabolical punishment, nails have been used since primitive times to release the demons believed to reside inside aching heads. Heave a sigh of gratitude that today we are spared such primitive medical treatments.

For his soul-body suffering, Jesus seeks relief not from nails, leeches, or crushed willow bark, but in the conviction that if he endured suffering like the dying grain of wheat, he would produce the kind of fruit that glorifies God. The Sufi mystic Rumi, quoted last Thursday, says of suffering: "Your defects are the ways that glory is manifested. Don't turn your head. Keep looking at the bandaged place. That is where the light enters you." Find relief from your pain in this wisdom that your wounds of heart and body are portholes through which the splendorous Light enters you. Keep in mind that your wounds and defects may very well be manifestations of the glory of God.

THE FIFTH WEEK OF LENT

Monday of the Fifth Week in Lent

Using pulverized willow bark to treat fever and headaches had the negative side effects of gastrointestinal irritation and bleeding. In 1893, Felix Hoffman, a young German chemist, seeking some relief for his father's painful rheumatoid arthritis, experimented with a synthetic form of willow bark. It worked, giving relief to his father. The young chemist's employer, the German drug company Bayer, named his discovery aspirin. It became the world's most prescribed drug and over a century later scientists do not entirely know why aspirin is such an effective painkiller, fever reducer, and anti-inflammatory agent. In recent years, an aspirin a day has been prescribed to aid in prevention of strokes and heart disease.

Heart problems increase with age because as we get older, the tissues of our body, and especially the muscles of our heart, lose their ability to quickly repair and regenerate themselves after damage. With each decade of life our blood pressure tends to increase. The rise in this pressure is due to increased stiffness in our blood vessels, which inhibits the normal flow of blood, causing strokes, heart failures, and angina.

The heart, as we are reminded every Valentine's Day, is also used to depict the font of emotions and love. With age, this heart can also suffer from inflexibility. The stiffening of our heart restricts the flow of new or different ideas and causes an inability to embrace change, since those so afflicted are "set in their ways." Aging hearts easily suffer a decline in zest and enthusiasm and are candidates for soul-stroke, joyless pessimism, and cynicism. In Sunday's first reading this week, Jeremiah speaks of a cardiac procedure performed by God: "I will put my law within them and I will write it on their hearts; and I will be their God, and they shall be my people" (Jer 31:33). What God has written on our hearts is a covenant, a marriage contract.

Regardless of your age, whenever you feel a heart attack of cynicism, a rigid rejection of something new just because it seems novel, or if you experience a blockage in your circulation of compassion, don't take an aspirin! Instead, take your fingers and move them slowly across your heart, reading, Braille-like, the words written by God upon it. The covenant is encapsulated in one word, so prayerfully move from letter to letter: "L-O-V-E." That word, one of the divine names, is a summation of what can bring healing to you and to the world.

Today's prescription for overall wellness and for a daily rejuvenation of a youthful and flexible heart is to trace your finger over those four blessed letters of your marriage contract with your Beloved that are inscribed upon your heart.

THE FIFTH WEEK OF LENT

TUESDAY OF THE FIFTH WEEK IN LENT

Clinical research has shown that there is healing power in reducing the amount of attention paid to the bodily sensations of our aches and pains. It seems that the more attention we pay to them, the more we experience the pain of our symptoms. For example, continuously thinking of how dry and scratchy my throat feels causes me to cough more often.

Aspirin and other pain drugs act like roadblocks on the neural pathways to the brain. Today's prescription for the next time you wish to alleviate some pain you're experiencing is not to use an aspirin-type roadblock but, rather, to take a detour—by practicing mindless suffering. In being as absent-minded as possible about an affliction, you may be surprised at the degree of relief you experience. Pain captures our attention; so try intentionally diverting your mind away from it by becoming engrossed in a book, in a conversation, or in the problems of others. Next week's Passion of Jesus provides some poignant examples of this kind of pain relief. In the midst of his all-encompassing suffering, Jesus comforted the weeping women of Jerusalem, showed concern for the needs of his mother and John, and extended compassion to his fellow crucified prisoners. This must have provided for him islands of relief from the excruciating pain of his cross and passion.

Buddha taught that with our thoughts we make our worlds, and science confirms that. Our world is pain-filled when our mind is occupied only with our pain. We can practice mindless therapy any time we itch all over from impatience, any time we are feverishly angry over some insult or affront, or when we are bored nearly to death by a dull homily or conversation. As with all medicines, today's prescription for healing can also be deadly when taken in excess or when used inappropriately. For example, we can misuse this medicine by mindlessly diverting our attention away from others' pain of poverty, homelessness, prejudice, or other social evils.

We can also fall into the malpractice of mindless violence, which itself is becoming an acute crippling disease in our society. Mindless violence is a term that Suzanne Stabile used for the unrecognized abuse we inflict on ourselves by being overcommitted. As we've already seen, violence is a staple in sports, motion pictures, video games, and the news. Thomas Merton confirms Suzanne Stabile's diagnosis about this invisible form of violence: "To allow oneself to be carried away by a multitude of conflicting concerns, to surrender to too many demands, to commit oneself to too many projects, to want to help everyone in everything is to succumb to violence."

What makes this virus so deadly to our soul-body is that the excessive busyness caused by striving to respond to every need and good project is often sanctified as the admirable quality of selfless service. So, on this lenten Tuesday, give your agenda a medical checkup to see if you are afflicted with the

THE FIFTH WEEK OF LENT

virus of mindless violence. If you are, begin your treatment by immediately taking out your scalpel and cutting back on your commitments.

THE FIFTH WEEK OF LENT

℞ WEDNESDAY OF THE FIFTH WEEK IN LENT

The second most common reason for visiting doctors is back and neck pain, following closely upon respiratory illnesses, like flu and the common cold. Eighty percent of Americans will experience the agony of back pain sometime in their lives. As we Americans become more sedentary, neglect exercise, grow even more overweight, and accelerate our ever-increasingly stressful lifestyle, back and neck pain will likely become even more prevalent. Relief is sought through surgery, pain pills, acupuncture, yoga, massage, chiropractic treatments, and that frightening prescription, "You'll just have to learn to live with it."

As crowded as doctor's offices are with this problem, a common job-related complaint not taken to any physician is having "a pain in the neck." Seventy percent of workers polled reported suffering from this kind of pain, which is made all the more acute because its source is a relationship from which they can't escape. "A pain in the neck" is a polite euphemism for the pain located in another part of the body. It is brought on by an irritation caused by an annoying coworker, the boss, or a family member. When forced to take the prescription,

"You'll just have to live with it," the stress created by bottling up emotions very often causes actual physical pain.

Dr. John Sarno of the NYU medical center is convinced that outside of arthritic or other orthopedic difficulties, most common back pains are caused by bottled-up emotions and repressed rage. The source of this intensely detrimental emotional constipation could be betrayal by a friend; sexual, physical, or psychological abuse; family crises; problems connected with a job; or any number of other common struggles. Dr. Sarno believes the fermenting stress of suppressed anger and resentment creates mild oxygen privation that creates muscle spasm, numbness, and pain not only in the back but also elsewhere in the body. He believes that "pain is created by the brain to make sure that the rage doesn't come out."

Although Dr. Sarno's pain theories have not yet been scientifically proven, Jesus confirms his diagnosis that suppressed rage is deadly. The Galilean Healer may well have prescribed, "Never let the sun set on your anger." Being a realist, he knew that anger can explode as spontaneously as fire and is just as deadly if it is not extinguished as quickly as possible. Even the everyday irritation of a minor resentment toward another needs emergency treatment. Jesus warned that harboring hateful thoughts toward another makes us liable to the judgment of murder! Aware of the dire consequences of intense anger, make an appointment to visit Doctor Jesus on this late-lenten Wednesday.

THE FIFTH WEEK OF LENT

THURSDAY OF THE FIFTH WEEK IN LENT

The daughter of the healer god Aesculapius was Hygeia, the goddess of health, and her symbol is a serpent drinking from a bowl. From her name comes our term for healthy living and preventive medicine. Good hygiene includes proper exercise, a good diet, and frequent hand washing to help prevent the spread of illness. Similarly, good hygiene of the soul includes a healthy sense of humor. The ability to laugh at ourselves, our missteps, and the hardships of life cleanses us from the virus of self-importance.

Humor creates a therapeutic corrective vision, allowing us to see around the corner, to see the funny side of any situation. Humorous vision assists our escape from the prison of a narrow perspective—from being locked into only one side, often the negative side, of any difficulty. Comedy tempers pride. Evil, lacking this gift of the gods, finds humor repulsive, and so lightheartedness is the most effective way to exorcise the demon of prideful stubbornness. Pride doesn't allow for laughing at ourselves and our pompous foibles, and so humor can lead to the therapeutic somersault cure of turning upside down with laughter whatever we consider deadly serious. Health warning: "Excessive seriousness can be sickening—it is a clear danger to your health."

Margot Adler, who could be called a spiritual pharmacist, prescribes "a really rich fantasy life so you can image what the possibilities are and a sense of humor so you can deal with what is." A healthy fantasy life contributes to good hygiene because it allows us to imagine a better future toward which we can set our sights. When you're faced with a crippled, unfulfilled life, be your own pharmacist and mix up a healing batch of fantasy and hope. By imaging a desired future that is better than your present life, you've created an inner blueprint and so have already started to give that future life. Now you can add a large dose of hope to that dream of a happier life and a pledge that with sacrifice and the help of God, you can begin to achieve it.

The necessary ingredient of hope isn't an idle yearning but an expectation based on remembrance. Hope flows from the memory of God's design for a promised land sown in the seeds of the Passover and in the promise of a new age of justice, peace, and true equality present in the seeds of the Lord's Supper. Add to these memories of God's graced interventions in times past those acts of divine involvement in your own personal life. Recall the numerous times you have been given good things, when you have been rescued and liberated, and let these memories reanimate your hope for the present and the future. Similar to the three cardinal virtues of faith, hope, and charity, the three therapeutic virtues are hope, humor, and a rich fantasy life.

THE FIFTH WEEK OF LENT

Friday of the Fifth Week in Lent

Since next Friday is Good Friday, let us return to the notion of nails as agents of healing. When what was thought to be the cross of Jesus was found just outside Jerusalem, the nails used to crucify him were also said to have been unearthed. They were encased in golden, jeweled reliquaries and became powerful relics that were said to heal the sick and crippled in medieval times. The sick came in droves to the cathedrals that housed these powerful relics. At least twenty-four nails were venerated as the authentic nails of Christ's passion!

Four nails are found in the earliest depictions of the cross, often shown with one at each corner of the cross. By the Middle Ages, however, paintings of the crucifixion showed only three nails—one for each hand and one nailing together the two feet. The Gypsies have a story to explain the missing nail. They say that on that first Good Friday, a Gypsy passing Calvary stole one of the nails to spare Jesus at least a little pain. In gratitude for this effort to alleviate some of his suffering, Jesus granted all Gypsies the right to steal from non-Gypsies when necessary!

The Fifth Week of Lent

In preparation for Good Friday and as a rule of life, consider becoming like that good Gypsy, who at every opportunity attempts to steal a nail so as to spare Christ a bit of pain. This is much more than a mere pious suggestion. Rather, it is the flip side of Paul's encouraging us to embrace our pain as a sharing in the suffering of Christ's Passion. While he was still a zealous persecutor of the original disciples of Jesus, Saul had a blinding vision while traveling the road to Damascus. Out of the blinding light a voice said, "Saul, Saul, why do you persecute me? I am Jesus, whom you are persecuting" (Acts 9:4–5).

Christ is persecuted again when we persecute others; he is nailed again and again as we inflict pain upon others. Today and every day is Good Friday, where the nailing of Christ is repeated at ten thousand street corner Calvaries. The twenty-four pious nail relics of the crucifixion were but a microscopic collection of the millions of nails with which Christ was, is, and will be crucified. The next time you are tempted to inflict pain on another, whether physically, verbally, or emotionally, see that desire as a large nail that you can either drive into the hand of Christ or one that you can steal away. Become a compassionate thief and steal as many nails as possible by refusing to use them to inflict pain. When, for example, you're in a group that is busy crucifying someone with the sharp nails of painful gossip or prejudicial remarks, become a crafty thief and steal their nails by changing the subject. Or you can become an audacious thief by blatantly challenging the spitefulness of prejudice. Each time you steal a nail, you share in Christ's Passion by participating in his healing, redemptive work. Steal at least one nail on this Friday before Good Friday.

THE FIFTH WEEK OF LENT

SATURDAY OF THE FIFTH WEEK IN LENT

A curious and astonishing phrase is tucked away in next Saturday's Easter Vigil liturgy: *Felix culpa,* meaning "O happy fault." This phrase barely raised an eyebrow in former times; its meaning often missed because it was sung in Latin. Yet, even today it slips beneath our spiritual radar when it is sung in English. Appearing in the midst of a long joyful canticle, the *Exsultet* or Easter Proclamation, this verse deserves prayerful pondering with delightful awe: "O happy fault, O necessary sin of Adam, which gained for us so great a Redeemer!"

Even speaking that phrase, "O happy fault," can be a shock to our spiritual sensibilities, since we typically beat our breast bewailing our sinful failings. Confession of sins is a traditional act before Easter, yet studies show that 50 percent of Catholics only go to confession once or twice a year. The studies further show that over 30 percent never celebrate the sacrament of reconciliation. Christ the Teacher calls us to forgive each other seventy-seven times, implying that forgiveness is a process rather than a one-time act of granting instant amnesty to the offender. Confession and reconciliation in or outside the sacramental celebration bring a healthy purging to one's soul.

Forgiving another person is an internal detoxification from the poison of hurt and anger caused by another. This healing process first requires draining the poisonous toxin of anger and then flushing one's soul with a flood of compassion for the person or life event that injured you. Forgiveness followed by reconciliation is the ultimate expression of Jesus' teaching on nonviolence. The Greek word for reconciliation, which is one of the primary healing works of Lent, literally means "making otherwise." It suggests a significant and drastic reversal from anger and hostile resentment to love and harmony.

Felix culpa—happy the fault of Adam! Happy also are our sins that have made it possible for Christ to restore us with healing love! Happy especially are our sins that you have opened to forgiveness, for they are infallible gauges and models of how we are to forgive others. Happy, too, are our sins that safeguard us from being haughty or disdainful of others who are guilty of sin. Be happy, then, that by the brokenness of our sinning we've become more beautiful than we ever were in our virginal, white, first communion innocence.

Japanese people greatly value their exquisite ceramic vases and do not throw them away when they are accidentally broken. Instead, they painstakingly glue together the broken pieces, filling the cracks with gold in a way that actually enhances the damage rather than hiding it. O blessedly happy are our sins by which we have become magnificently beautiful and by which we have been stunningly enhanced by God's golden love!

THE FIFTH WEEK OF LENT

HOLY
WEEK

PALM OR PASSION SUNDAY

Like modern drugstores, ancient pharmacies offered prophylactic medicines for protection against diseases. For the Egyptians, green palm branches were prophylactic shields placed on top of mummies to protect the deceased in the next world and to ensure eternal life. Miners used to carry small pieces of blessed palms in the shape of a cross as protection when they entered the dangerous bowels of the earth. Palm branches woven into crosses were placed in homes to ward off disease, pestilence, lightning, and demons. Farmers would place palm crosses in their fields to repel blights and ensure fertility. These and similar pious practices attribute almost magical powers to blessed palm branches which have long been considered signs of strength in adversity. Old legends hold that if a heavy weight is placed on top of a palm tree, it will still stand tall. This explains why Nike, the Greek goddess of victory, was believed to have rewarded palm branches to the victors for remaining strong in great conflict.

As Jesus is greeted with palm branches today while riding up into the Holy City, these famous lines from the poetry of Robert Frost could well be applied to him:

HOLY WEEK

Two roads diverged in a wood, and I—
I took the one less traveled by,
And that has made all the difference.
　　　　　—"The Road Not Taken"

The choice of the road that Jesus would travel was confirmed in the olive garden of Gethsemane. In fact, it was three years earlier, at his baptism, when he first chose that road. His "less traveled road" was the Way traveled by those marked with the *Tau,* the cross of those already living in the New Reign of the Age of God. Faithful to that cross, Jesus lived centuries—if not millennia—ahead of his time, and so his life set him apart from others. Because Jesus was a living lesson, people called him "Rabbi" (Teacher) and to all who found his lesson intriguing he said, "Come, follow me" (Lk 18:22) and invited them to become students of the Way.

That same invitation still thunders in the ears of all Jesus' disciples today. Indeed, it produces tremors of apprehension, if not outright fright, that the road less traveled will end on bloody Calvary! While tempted to bolt, however, do not detour onto that crowded "more traveled" road. Instead, remain faithfully beside Jesus as a good student during these days of Holy Week. By so doing, you will learn the art of healing your sufferings, pains, fears of shame, and the greatest of all fears—the fear of the incurable Eden's epidemic: death! In Gethsemane, Jesus reaffirmed the road that he would travel even though it would ultimately lead to his death. Today, boldly reaffirm your own baptismal decision to walk the road less traveled by tracing the *Tau* cross upon your forehead.

HOLY WEEK

MONDAY OF
HOLY WEEK

This Monday of Holy Week suggests that shame may
have been more excruciating for Jesus than the
nailing of his hands and feet to the cross. In Palestinian society
during his day, one's personal value was determined by one's
honor and undermined by one's shame. The loss of honor
could be as painful as death itself. What kind of relief might
Jesus have sought from the intense pain of being shamed?

Jesus, the prophet of Galilee, found inspiration in the
words of the prophet Isaiah, especially his prophecies about a
new era of peace and justice. The first five words in this quote
from Palm Sunday's first reading (Is 50:4–7) contain a
protective prescription for enduring the pain of suffering
shame:

> "The Lord God helps me;
> therefore I have not been disgraced;
> therefore I have set my face like flint,
> and I know that I shall not be put to
> shame."
>
> —Isaiah 50:7

Those five simple words, "The Lord God helps me,"
indicate the source of Jesus' power to stand tall as a palm tree

while being disgraced, slandered, ridiculed, abused, and even stripped naked by the Roman soldiers.

If these words are lived as an absolute truth, they become a shield to protect us from what we fear even more than cancer—censure! The specter of censure and criticism evoke a primal fear in us and exert a strong influence on our behavior and attitudes. The Chinese *Book of the Tao*, speaks of its effects: "Care about people's approval and you will be their prisoner." When we experience even mild disapproval, we endure shame. Jesus showed resistance to a strong dose of this affliction when he stood tall before rejection by his own people. He also was untouched by an even stronger dose of verbal abuse and ridicule when the scribes, Pharisees, and priests labeled him a dangerous and subversive preacher. His antibiotic shield rested in his profound conviction that God was his help. Jesus appears to have lived with the unshakable conviction that the Spirit of God possessed him. Enormous power flows from such certainty and that same power is available to you since, through Christ, the same Holy Spirit dwells within you!

As you reflect on the accounts of Jesus' passion during these days of Holy Week, find inspiration in his quiet confidence and strength in the midst of being shamed. Be motivated to live similarly, convinced that God is your help. Be assured that God is constantly at your side and that all you need to do is call out for help. Live, pray, and embrace the difficulties of life absolutely certain that the Spirit of divine approval and affirmation resides within you. Whenever you feel that others—even those in high places—are judging you, know that all judgments other than those of God are superficial and insignificant. Practice Jesus' five-word prescription for relief from shame and censure: "The Lord God helps me."

HOLY WEEK

TUESDAY OF HOLY WEEK

"**C**aution, Caution, Caution" is an appropriate prayer mantra for this Tuesday of Holy Week, since at long last Lent is ending, with tomorrow being the last full day of this pharmaceutical season. The remaining days of this week are called the *Triduum*, the three high holy days of the Lord's passion, death, and resurrection. Caution is required as your lenten retreat ends, for this is a time just as dangerous for you as it was for Jesus at the completion of his forty desert days of fasting. Satan the Tempter cunningly chose to tempt Jesus not at the beginning but at the end of his long retreat. Having accomplished the difficult feat of forty days of prayer and fasting, Jesus' feelings of achievement and pride are only natural.

Likewise as your lenten retreat ends, the Great Tempter can whisper in your ear: "Be proud of all the good you've accomplished this Lent, especially compared to others. You've been disciplined in personal prayer, fasting, attendance at lenten services, and in outreach to the poor. God is pleased and proud of what you've accomplished and you should be as well." The soul virus lurking during this week of weeks is pride—unholy vanity. But the end of Holy Week isn't a time to polish your halo; it's a time to be more vigilant than usual, for Satan cleverly uses our greatest strengths as the doorways for temptation, just as he did with Jesus.

The Tempter cleverly uses logic as a lure to ensnare you. Like a panting marathon runner who rejoices to see the finish line a short distance away, so you also may feel relieved that the labors of this long penitential season will be over tomorrow at sundown. In three short days, our lenten resolutions and disciplines will end, and with a song of "Alleluia" life will again return to normal. How clever that the hook is bated with the lure of logic: When the race is over, it's over! That's the Old Tempter's time-tested strategy that has worked for centuries to delay the coming of the Reign of God. As Saint Paul cautioned, "So if you think you are standing (like a palm tree), watch out that you do not fall" (1 Cor 10:12).

Lenten resolutions, like those of New Year's Day, can be placebos, relieving our itch to reform bad habits. Our lenten works can be a temporary salve for our mediocre prayer and lukewarm spirituality. Medicines usually have an expiration date and if on Ash Wednesday you set Easter as the expiration date for your works of reform, consider voiding that prescription timetable! Those who have taken up the cross are pledged to a *lifelong* reformation of removing faults and growing in prayer, justice, love of God, and love of neighbor.

HOLY WEEK

WEDNESDAY OF HOLY WEEK

This last full day of Lent, "Phoenix Wednesday," is
named after a fabled immortal bird and not for the
city in Arizona. Forty days ago was Ash Wednesday, the day
you began your lenten journey marked with the sign of ashes.
Let the season conclude with the sign of the phoenix. Since
antiquity, it was believed that as the death of a phoenix drew
near, the bird would construct a nest of spices and aromatic
twigs. Then, by intensely flapping its wings, it would ignite
the nest into a cremation inferno. Out of the ashes of this fire,
a bird of matchless splendor would arise—a bird much more
beautiful than the bird that had died.

In medieval times, the phoenix was a symbol of the
resurrected Christ, and as Lent ends, it can symbolize the
more beautiful person you have become after being
transformed more closely to Christ. *The Phoenix and the
Turtle* is a legend of the love between a phoenix and a
turtledove, the bird that symbolizes romantic love. In that
legend, death and love are wedded, just as they have been
during these past forty days of conversion, when out of love
you have died to the old you in order that a new you might
arise. The fire of love is the only authentic chemistry for
transforming imperfection into perfection. Any reformation

of self without a passionate love for God and all creation ultimately becomes destructive rather than life-giving.

Guilt can be a wholesome igniter of the desire to reform. Yet guilt and its conjoined twin, shame, can also fuel a fire of hatred toward your body and its natural desires. Out of that evil oven of shame and guilt comes deformity—not the healthy and holy transformation that is the goal of Lent. Only love powers the medicine of the Spirit by which our imperfections undergo purification. This holy chemistry returns us to our original state; it is a process of restoration, not immolation.

The gospel of "Phoenix Wednesday" is the overture for tomorrow's commemoration of the Lord's Supper, where something truly new arises, where a new covenanted bond of love is forged between God and humanity. Yet, we also need to keep in mind how Jesus identified his betrayer as someone seated near him at that table. For those who have taken up the cross, it would be an act of infidelity—a form of betrayal—to stop living a life of ongoing reform after Lent has come to an end. So, if you are tempted to return to your old ways and habits—or if you need to muster up some courage for the final phoenix-like cremation inferno of Lent—use the good medicine of the prayer-mantra, "the Lord God helps me." These concluding words of today's reading from the prophet Isaiah (Is 50:4–9) are just what the doctor ordered for committing to a phoenix faith life.

HOLY WEEK

THE PASCHAL TRIDUUM

Holy Thursday-Easter Sunday

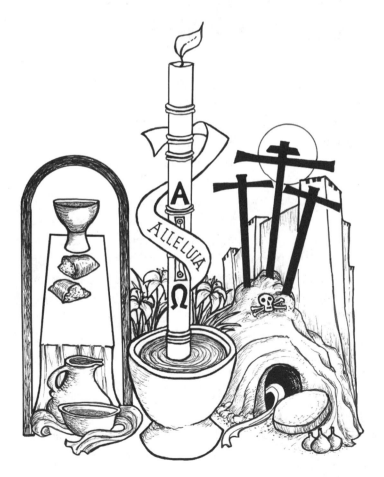

HOLY THURSDAY
Day of the Lord's Supper

Jesus gathers with his intimate friends in the upper room to celebrate a most special supper, although his friends are unaware that it will be the final meal they share with Jesus. He signals that this is the last by his invitation, "Do this in memory of me." Of all the many remembrances of it, tonight's Mass of the Lord's Supper holds the therapeutic power to heal our personal apathy at lethargic liturgies. The great theologian Karl Rahner once said: "We commonplace people make this mystery of eternal life so ordinary . . . the priest performs his office morosely, impelled by objective duty as though he was carrying out some chore." Rahner further describes our common malaise, saying that after receiving the Body of Christ we still return weary, taking the same heavy heart back home from the table of the God.

The healing gift of Holy Thursday is a new heart, an apathy-proof heart, which never tires of wondering at this marvel of love that we call the eucharist. The secret of such an ever-youthful eucharistic heart is to be awed by every gift of love. To be loved by another should always amaze us and

TRIDUUM

should never be taken for granted. Holy Thursday's supper is a supreme feast of love, and so it should be an occasion for us to express deep gratitude for all our gifts of love.

After giving thanks at the Last Supper, Jesus broke the bread, saying, "This is my body." Were those words a consecration of or an acknowledgment of a mystical reality, or perhaps both? Jesus pronounced those sacred words at the end of a life that expressed full union with God. And if he was one with God, then he was also one with all of God's creation, including wheat and grapes, bread and wine. Is it possible that to those who came to him with bodies diseased, crippled, or paralyzed he also said, "This is my body"? And to those whose bodies were sick with sin or covered with sores of shame, did he say, "This is my body?" Holy Thursday renews our sacred baptismal commission to continue living Jesus' admonition to "do this in memory of me," by also saying "This is my body" to the poor and the hungry, to our spouses, children, friends, strangers, and even our enemies.

There is a custom in Thailand that before a person dies, he or she collects several dozen favorite recipes in a booklet, which is then distributed to friends at the funeral. By continuing to prepare those recipes, they help the deceased person live on in their enjoyment of the delicious foods that their loved one had enjoyed in life. At the Last Supper Jesus did the same thing by passing on his all-encompassing recipe for the living feast of God's love which embodied the essence of his life on earth. So we should continue to remember and do as Jesus did.

TRIDUUM

GOOD FRIDAY
The Passion
and Death of Jesus

Since antiquity, a variety of pharmaceutical drugs have been used in the effort to relieve pain. Those who have endured excruciating pain like that caused by migraine headaches, advanced cancer, or severe burns have truly experienced Good Friday. The word "excruciating" is from the Latin *ex-cruciare*, meaning "of" or "from the cross (*crux*)." This expression describes well the pain that is as terrible as being crucified. Crucifixion was invented by the Persians and adopted by the Romans because it was the ultimate deterrent to disorder and rebellion. Leading to a slow death with a maximum of pain and suffering, crucifixion was the worst punishment possible. As such, it was reserved as a punishment for runaway slaves, soldiers who had deserted, and those who rebelled against the authority of Rome.

The hideous death of Jesus was a state-sanctioned execution endorsed by religious officials and the crowd. Each Good Friday, every crucifix or cross challenges those who support capital punishment. Remembering the passion and death of Jesus invites those who suffer excruciating pain of body or spirit to rename this day "Good Hope Friday."

TRIDUUM

On this day of the cross, hope for the coming of the Reign of God is also found in the words of Terrence MacSwiney, words which could easily have been spoken by the crucified Jesus: "It is not those who can inflict the most, but those who can suffer the most who will conquer." MacSwiney was the Lord Mayor of Cork, Ireland, who spoke these words while imprisoned in 1920 by the British for making revolutionary statements. He died in prison after a seventy-four day hunger strike, which he endured for the sake of Irish independence. The political structures of the British Empire were as unmoved by his death as were the Roman authorities by the death of Jesus of Galilee. The heroic death of MacSwiney became an inspiration for the Irish, much like the death of Jesus continues to inspire his disciples. The cross beckons us, even today, to labor always for the Reign of God.

"Good Hope Friday" celebrates the victory of those suffering excruciating pain who embrace with trust the conviction that their pain has meaning. Paradoxically, the cost of loving is excruciating pain; as the Master said, "No one has greater love than this, to lay down one's life for one's friends" (Jn 15:13). This sacrificial gift of life might involve a single, heroic act of dying for others or years of heroic, unrelenting sacrifice for the needs of others.

The spectators at Jesus' execution taunted him, saying, "He trusts in God; let God deliver him . . ." (Mt 27:43). While Jesus profoundly believed in Isaiah's words, "the Lord God helps me," at the most painful hour of his life, it seemed that his father in heaven had completely abandoned him. While to all outward appearances Jesus' dying prayer for help went unanswered, did not the Divine Physician answer it with the cure of Calvary? Along with all those slowly dying in excruciating physical and spiritual pain, did not Jesus finally find relief in surrendering even unto death?

TRIDUUM

HOLY "EGG" SATURDAY
Easter Eve

Today, also known as "Tomb Saturday," is observed as a solemn vigil at the tomb of Jesus, yet it is also a day of joyful preparation. Holy Saturday is busy with the preparation of festive foods, the dyeing of Easter eggs, and the cleaning and decorating of our homes in preparation for the great feast of Easter. After sunset tonight, the Easter Vigil is celebrated, during which the catechumens, after their long period of preparation, are initiated into the church through the sacraments of baptism, confirmation, and eucharist. They are born anew as Easter people.

Eggs are primary symbols of Easter, for they are nature's tomb-wombs, where behind the thinnest of membrane walls new life awaits birth. Eggs have also long been connected with Easter because in former times, along with meat, they were forbidden foods during Lent and so became special Easter treats. Today, Easter eggs are usually used primarily for decoration. Yet in pre-Christian antiquity, eggs were "good medicine." Since life slumbered within them, they were often used in mystic healing and fertility rites. Among the ancient holy stories of creation is one that tells about the earth being hatched from a giant cosmic egg; other myths likewise speak of the first living person being hatched from an egg.

The Egyptians buried their dead with eggs, both as nourishment during their process of rebirth and as medicinal food for life after death. Archaeological excavations of ancient burial sites have found clay eggs interned with the deceased as protective burial amulets. These discoveries lead us to wonder whether Nicodemus, when burying Jesus with costly spices, also left an egg in his tomb.

Today's cholesterol-consciousness has placed a warning label on eggs that says, "Handle with Care." Just as valid, however, would be a label that says, "Handle with Reverence," for eggs have long been considered sacramentals, or signs of the holy. Symbols of Easter joy, eggs have been colored with vegetable dyes or painted in various colors for centuries and used as festive decorations. Among the Slavic peoples they have been adorned with gold and silver. Family and friends exchanged decorated eggs as Easter gifts, and more elaborately embellished eggs were often saved as family heirlooms. One German custom called for the piercing and emptying of eggs. The hollow eggshells were then brightly painted and hung as Easter decorations on trees and shrubs. In other countries, it was the custom to bury a blessed egg just outside the wall of one's home to ward off disease, misfortune, and lightning. Perhaps these age-old customs should be resurrected; certainly the sacramental status of eggs should be revived.

An egg is an excellent icon for prayer. On this Holy Saturday, use an egg to reflect on the experience of being entombed, as was the body of Jesus. Prayerfully meditate on the image of yourself as dead and buried. While occasionally we may think of our own death, few of us ever picture ourselves entombed, for such a suffocating thought is too dreadful to consider. Today, let your icon egg heal you of the fear of being buried as you contemplate it with trust in Jesus' promise that you will be raised up with him. Realize that the walls of your future tomb are made of the thinnest of membranes, just like the delicate shell of your egg. Then, raise your icon egg to your ear and listen. In the silence, hear the infallible triumphant shout, "Alleluia! Christ is Risen—and you with him!"

TRIDUUM

EASTER SUNDAY
The Resurrection
of Jesus Christ

Years ago, Easter was a feast of riotous joy because it signaled the end of fasting, abstaining from meat, and from doing other lenten penances. You can rejoice today in the resurrection of Christ and in the fact that you are leaving the Hospital of Lent with a healing prescription for the unparalleled drug of wellness and wholesome living. Your prescription is for *Triduum*, which is Latin for "a space of three days." This is what we call sundown on Holy Thursday through Easter Sunday evening. The Galilean Pharmacist's recipe for making *Triduum* is to mix a compound of three healing ingredients: the Supper of the Lord, his Passion and Death, and his Resurrection.

Medicines frequently carry the instruction, "Take with food," and this is especially true for your *Triduum* prescription. At each meal, take a moment of your time before you begin eating to relish the memory of Jesus, who by his love transformed all meals into occasions of holy communion. Before your family Easter dinner, you might want to renew an old table ritual. A parent blesses a hard-boiled Easter egg and then cracks open the shell and cuts the egg into pieces that are

TRIDUUM

divided among the members of the household. Each person then eats a section of the egg in silence, aware of the Easter promise of safety. The tradition says that if later in life any member of the household should get lost, all she or he has to do is remember the ritual of the shared egg. The rest of the household would then think of the lost member and their love-filled thoughts would guide that person safely home again.

Like a good pharmacist, next mix into the *Triduum* medicine the healing ingredient of Jesus' death on the cross. Remembering the innocence of the crucified Jesus can give us the grace to endure all the undeserved, excruciating pain that may be our fate in life. Enduring all our struggles is elevated to a state of grateful communion when our suffering is made meaningful by being wedded to the cross of Christ. Pour into this mixture a pint of Easter joy and stir it with the knowledge that the resurrection of Jesus proved that death does not have the last word! This Easter ingredient of faith that death and sin are not the end treats the great lifelong disease that plagues us all, the insatiable cancer of sin—that spiritual death—that slowly, inexorably nibbles away at body and mind. Sin deforms our souls as it kills our dreams of richly fulfilling marriages and our ideals of social and religious reform. Whenever you face any deaths like these, mark upon yourself the Easter cross, the *Tau* cross of those who already live fully in the promised age of God where sin and death have been destroyed.

The third medicinal ingredient that completes the prescription for *Triduum* is the mystery of God resurrecting Jesus. The crucified carpenter wasn't slumbering in his tomb—he was dead and decaying. In the great Easter Mystery, the Spirit of Life breaks open the stone egg of Jesus' tomb. Bursting forth from the shattered shell of this tomb-egg came new creation, a new earth, and a new Jesus who arose in stunning splendor. The power of that Easter event continues to transform the past, saturate the present, and create the future. Easter isn't merely a holy historical remembrance; it is a sacred encounter with the risen Christ who continues to heal as the ever-gentle savior.

Today we seek healing for our Easter itch, a subterranean doubt that we shall experience resurrection because of our failures and stumbling efforts to live the gospel. Before his death, Jesus gave a promise reassuring all who have struggled to live as he wanted us to live: "This is the will of him who sent me, that I should lose nothing of all that he has given me, but raise it up on the last day" (Jn 6:39). To reinforce these reassuring resurrection words of Jesus, *The Lenten Pharmacy* concludes with an ancient prescription: the medicine of a good story or parable. I am grateful to author Patricia Sanchez for the following story as a curative for the Easter itch.

After committing suicide for betraying Jesus, Judas found himself in pitch-black darkness at the bottom of an endlessly deep pit. After weeping for a thousand years in sorrow for his sinful betrayal, and now empty of tears, he looked up to see a tiny speck of light way up at the top of the black pit. After hundreds of years of contemplating that tiny glimmering glow, he attempted to climb up toward the light. For many more years he struggled to scale the slimy, slippery walls of that pit, only to lose his grip and come slithering down to the bottom. Finally, after several more lengthy attempts, he was able to crawl inch-by-inch all the way up to the rim at the top. Climbing out of the dark pit, he found to his surprise that he was in a luminously brilliant room where twelve men were seated at a long table. "We've been waiting for you, friend

TRIDUUM

Judas," said Jesus, who was seated at the far end, "we couldn't begin until you came."

This Easter, rest assured that Jesus waits for all of us with just as much patience and healing love. Let his all-powerful medicine of selfless love heal you and bring you new life.

TRIDUUM

Edward Hays, author of over thirty books on contemporary spirituality, has been a Catholic priest in the archdiocese of Kansas City, Kansas since 1958. He has served as director of Shantivanam, a Midwest center of contemplative prayer, and as a chaplain of the state penitentiary in Lansing. He has spent extended periods of pilgrimage in the Near East, the Holy Land, and India. He continues his ministry as a prolific writer and painter in Leavenworth, Kansas.

More Lenten Resources from Edward Hays

A Lenten Hobo Honeymoon
Lent calls each of us to be hobos, Homeward Bound pilgrims who cannot rest until we rest in God, our final destination. With insight, art, and a touch of humor, Fr. Hays guides us along a Lenten way that takes no short-cuts while at the same time making the way a honeymoon, a joy-filled journey with God homeward to God.
ISBN: 0-939516-43-8 / 143 pages / $12.95

The Ascent of the Mountain of God
In brief but powerful reflections for the 40 days of Lent, Fr. Hays has cre-ated a thought-provoking adventure, taking us on a sacred mountain climbing expedition. Beginning on Ash Wednesday, we are led to succes-sive heights on the way to the summit of the Easter mystery. A rich collec-tion of parables and stories for turning the challenge of the Lenten ascent into a joyful adventure.
ISBN: 0-939516-28-4 / 133 pages / $12.95

The Lenten Labyrinth
The journeys of Lent and of life are seldom straight roads but are usually like complicated labyrinths. While we often can feel lost along the com-plex twisting patterns of the labyrinth path, to travel the Way of Lent and of life is the greatest of all adventures. This guidebook of daily reflections has the power to change – to radically enrich – our way of thinking, loving, and believing.
ISBN: 0-939516-22-5 / 127 pages / $12.95

The Pilgrimage Way of the Cross
A creative blending of traditional stations along with new ones that reflect the complete Paschal Mystery of the Risen Christ. Readers are guided on a day-by-day pilgrimage experience of visiting the sites of the passion of Christ in and around the Holy City. Illustrated with pencil drawings, pho-tographs, and detailed maps.
ISBN: 0-939516-68-3 / 247 pages / $15.95
